GARLAND STUDIES ON

THE ELDERLY IN AMERICA

edited by
STUART BRUCHEY
UNIVERSITY OF MAINE

A GARLAND SERIES

THE OLDER WOMAN: THE ABLE SELF

———————

KATHLEEN DEE AHERN

GARLAND PUBLISHING, Inc.
New York & London / 1996

Library of Congress Cataloging-in-Publication Data

Ahern, Kathleen Dee, 1945–
    The older woman : the able self / Kathleen Dee Ahern.
        p.   cm. — (Garland studies on the elderly in America)
    Includes bibliographical references and index.
    ISBN 0-8153-2333-6
    1. Aged women—United States—Psychology. 2. Aging—United
States—Psychological aspects. 3. Self-reliance in old age—United
States. 4. Social surveys—United States. I. Title. II. Series.
HQ1064.U5A6377 1996   95-51444
305.26—dc20

Printed on acid-free, 250-year-life paper
Manufactured in the United States of America

This book is dedicated to the memory of my parents
Patricia L. and Francis A. Dee

Contents

Preface

This book is a result of the many years of experience I have had in caring for older women. My years as a nursing professor of community health afforded me the opportunity to visit many older women within the natural environment of their homes. From these visits I began to question how meaning was found in activity and to look beyond functional status. The focus on the over age 85 group came from my research which identified this group as the fastest growing older age group in the United States today. As the population continues to age, the problems that are encountered by families will increase. Family systems have undergone major shifts with restructured families the rule rather than an exception. These changes have resulted in fewer family members available to assist with elder care. The burden often falls upon adult children who have many other responsibilities related to work and dependent children. This book may be helpful to families who are struggling to understand the needs of older women.

It also contains a great deal of information related to the background for the study as well as how the data were obtained and interpreted. The first three chapters may be particularly helpful for individuals who wish to engage in grounded theory research or who are interested in the process. Chapter II has been organized to present relevant literature, in areas of functional activity, economics and gender issues. Chapter III provides a good review of the grounded theory method and many specific examples of how the data analysis was conducted. The reader who wishes to focus on the stories that these women told may focus on Chapter IV. It is in this chapter that the core of the study rests and one need not have any particular knowledge of research in order to understand the presentation. The words of the women were analyzed and grouped into themes which may be read in part or in whole depending on the needs of the reader.

To supplement the actual words of the women, the reader has been provided with short vignettes of their lives which are contained in appendix A. These vignettes provide important insights into the lives of these women and may be read prior to the rest of this book or after.

The older women in this study identified many needs especially in regards to improved family communication and community services. Contained within the study results are examples of many ways that families, professionals and society are failing to meet the needs of this growing population. There are many opportunities for professionals to become politically involved in issues related to services provided for older persons within the community. It is hoped that the words of these women will provide an impetus for health care professionals to address how the lives of older women can be improved.

Acknowledgments

The older women who so willingly shared their lives with me are thanked for making this book possible. I am deeply grateful to Dr. Judith Ackerhalt, Chair of my Dissertation Committee, for her friendship, guidance and support throughout my doctoral studies and to the faculty of Adelphi University. I have been fortunate to have the support of friends throughout this process. I am particularly grateful for the friendship of Allan Weidenbaum, Kathleen Rommel, Angela Moran and my long time friend, Nancy Nelsen. The nursing staff and Gloria Lonz-Miglionica of CCU at Staten Island University Hospital have supported me and assisted me to stay "grounded" in the real world. My colleagues at Wagner College, in particular Julia Barchitta, Ann Marie Sortino and Margo Governo are thanked for friendship and encouragement. During much of my doctoral studies, I served in the Army Reserve Nurse Corps. My fellow officers, especially Lt. Col. F. Swartz not only inspired me but also provided guidance and humor. I wish to acknowledge the following physicians: Dr. J. Kalman, Dr. V. Montanti, Dr. C. Vonfrolio and Dr. F. Forte for their friendship and care

My children, Jim and Sandra deserve a special thank you for all the love and support they have given me over this long process.

Finally, I am most grateful for the friendship and love of my husband Jim who has supported me through the best of times and the worst of times.

The Older Woman:
The Able Self

I

Introduction

In the United States, a major trend noted over the past four decades has been a marked increase in the growth of the elderly population, particularly those 85 and over. This group, which numbers approximately 3.2 million, represents a 50% increase since 1970. By the year 2000, the figure can be expected to reach 4.6 million. At that time, 71% of this population will be women age 85 or older as compared with 63% in 1990 (U.S. Bureau of Census 1992).

The elderly cannot be viewed as a homogenous group. People 65-75 years of age clearly have different problems than those age 85 and over. The latter, who tend to live alone, are more likely to have physical disabilities and chronic illnesses (Taeuber 1991). These factors contribute significantly to the vulnerablility of this age group and affect the way in which they function on a daily basis as contrasted with the elderly below age 85. While theories of aging have focused on the activities of the elderly, there has been no definitive agreement on one unifying theory. The basis for considering activity as a central focus for examining the process of aging can be attributed to the work of Viktor Frankl (1985) who notes that humans must respond by action to life. The actions of individuals afford them an opportunity to find meaning. Thus, activity can become a source of meaning in life.

The term *meaning* has been interpreted in various ways among different disciplines (Creelman 1966). How it is used would seem to be a determining factor as well as the context within which it appears. In exploring the term, Ogden and Richards (1953) suggest that meaning best can be understood when other words that are synonymous (for example intention, value, referent or emotion) are substituted. Frankl's (1986) approach is to define meaninglessness — an existential vacuum or a state without the realization of values. He explains his view as follows:

> Men can give meaning to their lives by realizing what I call creative values, by achieving tasks. But they can also give meaning to their lives by realizing experiential values, by experiencing the Good, the True and the Beautiful or by knowing one single human being in all his uniqueness. But even a man who finds himself in the greatest distress in which neither activity nor creating can bring values to life nor experience give meaning to it, even such a man can still give his life a meaning by the way he faces his fate, his. This possibility exists to the very last moment. I call such values attitudinal values. (p.xix)

The finding of meaning in one's life is a unique task requiring a constant search. The more the individual seeks the task of life, the more meaningful it will appear. Frankl views the goal as an actualization of values, in which the life tasks of the individual can be discovered.

Many studies have dealt with activity as a phenomenon. The word *activity* is derived from the Latin *activite*, which is defined as being active, exertion of energy and liveliness. Further interpretations include "to act is to drive, to be brisk and to do." (Partridge 1977, p.5). Activity also appears as movement in the disciplines of psychology, sociology, biology and philosophy (Blumer 1969; Bruner 1979; Johnson 1987; Polanyi 1962).

The concept of activity raises questions as to how it can be studied in older women without implying a sense of briskness or liveliness and getting things done. Furthermore, researchers on activity emphasize the empirical method of studying what is observable and measurable. This approach is questionable since the "doing" is neither readily observed in the elderly nor measured. Another issue is how does the elderly person continue to find meaning when the doing is less "brisk and energetic" and there appears to be less to do.

Major studies of activity in the older age groups have not considered the vast differences between people age 65 to 75 and those 85 and over. The focus has been on functional activities related to daily living (Katz and Stroud 1989; Lawton 1991; Manton 1988;

Rubenstein et al 1989). While the findings suggest that functional ability is related to maintaining independence, no direct relationship between functional ability and life satisfaction has been demonstrated.

There appears to be, however, a general decline in physical activity. Williams and Bird (1992) studied locomotion in healthy older and younger adults and concluded an inevitable slowing of the maximum output of the motor system. This decline in physical activity remains unexplored in relation to its meaning to individuals over age 85.

Little agreement has resulted on what activities should be examined and how they may be interpreted. In general, studies have used such divisions as passive and active, informal and formal, required and unrequired, social and solitary, and indoors and outdoors (Aniansson, Rundgren and Sperling 1980; Cauley, La Port, Sandler, Schiamm and Kristea 1987; Ford, Folmar, Solomon, Medalie and Galazka 1988; Heinemann, Colorez, Frank, and Taylor 1988; Lombranz, Bergman, Eyal and Shmotkin 1988; Katz and Stroud 1989). Different activities may be grouped under one study as active and another as social thus creating some ambiguity, with the interpretation left to the researcher.

Although women comprise the majority of persons age 85 and over, few studies of the older population have accounted for gender differences. Women have been almost invisible in investigations of older persons. Studies that focused on the experiences of men have generalized their findings to women. Harding (1986) notes that a major lack in   the research done is that it reports the nature of women and their activities disproportionately as they are experienced by men. This view is also supported by Hall (1985), who observes that what has appeared legitimately as knowledge, until recently, has been based not on human experience but on male experiences seen through male eyes.

Harding and Hintikka (1983) also cite the following concern about the use of male experiences as a basis for understanding those of women:

> What counts as knowledge must be grounded in experience. Human experience differs according to the kinds of activities and social relations in which humans engage.Women's experience systematically differs from the male experience upon which knowledge claims have

been grounded. Thus the experience on which the prevailing claims to social and natural knowledge are found is first of all, only partial human experience only partially understood: namely masculine experience as understood by men. (p.x)

Women spend a great deal of their lives being supportive and engaging in activities such as listening and giving non verbal support. They have traditionally built a sense of self worth on activities that they define as taking care of and giving to others (Miller 1986). A review of activity studies reveals that these activities are usually not included. When they are, however, they appear in such a way that the information relating to them cannot be easily interpreted.

Tinsley, Teoff, Colbs, and Kaufman (1985) studied leisure activites, which included reading and volunteer services; yet they omitted activities such as listening, relating or offering support. Peppers (1976) included visiting friends in his study but left out activities carried out in the process. Lawton (1987) cited helping others but placed it under an a obligatory category with housework. Cauley et al. (1987) identified homemaking as a physical activity while omitting any non physical activity, such as listening to others.

A major focus for women has been activities connected to the home (Oakely 1974). Women have traditionally assumed responsiblity for the care of the home whether or not they have engaged in outside work (United Nations 1991). Activity studies frequently have excluded work inside the home which may have much value for the older woman. Of interest is that, when housework or homemaking has been included, discrepancies occurred in how it should be categorized and interpreted. Devault (1990) notes that housework doesn't quite fit under work or leisure. This observation is supported by Harding (1986), who points out that for wives and mothers housework is neither wage labor nor a self directed activity.

Their exclusion from research has devalued women and their activities. This has been most evident with older women. Even the women's movement, which has focused on the needs of women, has neglected the older individual. Macdonald and Rich (1983) contend that it is as if the older women were indeed too depressing or an embarrassment to us beyond the reach of feminist analysis. This present research is an attempt to fill this void and explore the lives of an understudied population, women age 85 and over.

BEGINNING THE PROCESS

Purpose of the Study

The purpose of this study is to describe how women age 85 and over create meaning in their lives through activity. The following research questions are addressed:
1. How do women age 85 and over define activity?
2. What are the activities of women age 85 and over?
3. How do their activities help them create meaning in their lives?

Definition of Terms

Meaning — A state within which there is realization of values. It can be accomplished through creative values by achieving tasks, experiential values by experiencing and by attitudinal values- the attitude with which the individual faces suffering or distress in life. The search for meaning is a distinctive characteristic of being human (Frankl 1985).

Activity — Basically movement within a body cell or the movement of an individual engaging in a set of actions. Activity also involves experiencing, such as perceiving, interpreting or responding. These acts may not be observable but nonetheless reflect an active process.

Assumptions — are based upon constructs related to meaning, the individual, and acting. The primary assumption upon which the study rests is that life holds a potential meaning for each individual. Activities are interpreted as opportunities to create meaning and, therefore, are active processes.

Limitations

1. The sample was limited to females. Women comprise approximately two thirds of the aging population and according to forecasts will continue to do so (U.S. Bureau of Census 1992). However, they have been and continue to be an understudied population. Research has usually included only men. When women have been included, insufficient data have been gathered on gender differences.

2. The sample was limited to women age 85 and over. The age group 85 and over constitutes one of the fastest growing segments of the population. Studies have not often separated out this age group from others 65 years and older. This lack results in an inaccurate depiction of the age group 85 and over which has different characteristics.

3. The sample was limited to women who were alert, oriented, and able to understand instructions. The level of orientation required was an awareness of self, location, and month. Orientation to day or time of day was not required.

4. The present sample was limited to women living in the community. This selection was consistent with the finding that 75% of women age 85 and over reside in the community. (Herzog in Herzog et al (1989)

Significance of Study

This study is significant because it explores an understudied population, women age 85 and over. Because of the increasing numbers of women in this age bracket, it is important for members of the health care community to understand how these individuals make sense of their lives.

Marked differences exist among older individuals that are not accounted for when persons over age 85 are studied in the same sample with those 65 and over. Therefore, the present study's focus provides a needed perspective on older women.

Although the body of knowledge related to functional activities has offered effective tools for planning the health needs of older individuals, the research has not shown the individual's view of those activities and activity itself. The empirical pattern dominates studies of activities. While the measurements may appear valuable, they do not permit the meaning of activities to emerge. The qualitative approach of this study allowed women to express in their own words how they conducted their activities and what meanings they held for them.

The activities of women have differed from those of men in that the former have assumed the role of caretakers of the home whether or not employed in outside work. Since many activity tools omit work inside the home, women may score falsely low on productive activity. Also omitted have been other activities that require a great deal of a woman's time such as listening and providing support to others. Activity studies, therefore, reveal an empirical perspective non-inclusive of women.

The present study has implications for professionals because it provides new knowledge about a large, growing population with multiple health needs. Information about how women 85 years and older live their lives on a daily basis can help professionals in planning care in acute and long term care facilities as well as in the home.

By learning how these older women create meaning in their lives through activity, we will be able to assist other older women to learn how to cope with chronic disease and disablilities

The Method

The methodology selected for this study was qualitative, which seeks to gain insight through discovering the meanings attached to a given phenomenon (Burns and Grove 1987). Qualitative research refers to the methods and techniques of observing, analyzing, and interpreting attributes, patterns, characters and meanings of specific, contextual or gestaltic features of phenomena under study (Leininger 1985). The focus of this method is holistic, using inductive reasoning (Burns and Grove 1987). It is descriptive research concerned with process rather than just outcomes or products. Meaning becomes an essential concern. Researchers employing this approach are interested in the ways different people make sense out of their lives (Bogden and Bilken 1982).

The qualitative method allows for the researcher to be closely involved in the study. It provides a unique opportunity for the experiences of a woman to emerge, particularly when the researcher is a female. The approach is sound with interviewing as a technique for data gathering. The process of a woman interviewing women can be an effective as well as an essential way of giving the subjective situation of women greater visability (Roberts 1988).

The utilization of a female researcher with female subjects is encouraged by Acker (in Stromberg and Harkess 1988), who notes that bias often appears in studies by male researchers with preconceived notions when studying women.

Qualitative research has been used for many years in the social sciences but is relatively new to the health professions. It has particular meaning as these professions struggle with concepts related to quality of life issues. This method allows the researcher flexibility and an opportunity to view holistically the problem under study. In research on the older woman, its humanistic approach provides a framework for promoting a better understanding of the participants.

Grounded theory uses an inductive, from the ground up approach employing everyday behaviors or organized patterns to generate theory (Hutchinson 1993). Concerned with process, it is considered an appropriate method when little is known about a topic or few adequate theories exist to explain or predict a group's behavior. Since the purpose of this study was to explain a process, the grounded theory method was selected.

II

Literature Review

THE BACKGROUND

Research Perspective

Theory, as characterized by Glaser and Strauss (1967) is a strategy for describing and explaining some phenomenon. It is generated by the scientist from the data and thus remains connected to or grounded in that data (Stern 1980). Most hypotheses and concepts that evolve are systematically worked out during the research process.

This study employed grounded theory as a qualitative method to discover theory from data, there is no attempt to use concepts and relationships from theory. The research can be guided within a framework aimed to foster data inquiry and collection (Miles and Huberman 1984).

An existentialist framework, based on Viktor Frankl's theory of meaning in life, has guided the present investigation. It has provided a broad focus designed to direct but not to predict the outcomes of the research. Frankl (1985), who has studied the human search for meaning in life, based his theory on the premise that life has meaning and is available to everyone. He also noted that life retains its meaning under any conditions.

His theory is founded on two main propostions — the will to meaning and a meaning to life. He describes the deep seated striving and struggle for a higher ultimate meaning to existence. Life is never lacking in meaning, with each situation unique. It is the individual's responsibility to seek the meaning, even in the most hopeless situations. These views of Frankl emanate largely from his experiences as a prisoner in concentration camps (Frankl 1985).

This theory is applicable to an older population in light of Frankl's belief that life has meaning until the very end. He proposes that "when we are no longer able to change a situation, we are challenged to change ourselves" (Frankl 1985, p.43). Elderly women must cope with many changes in their lives, created by increasing dependence, chronic illness, and different environments.

Meaning to life can emerge by recognizing values in the creative, experiential and attitudinal realms. Frankl (1986) describes them as follows:

> 1. Creative values — These are realized by achieving tasks, doing or creating. This may be through one's work or occupation.
> 2. Experiential values — The person acts to respond or experience. This would be a situation such as loving or watching a sunset.
> 3. Attitudinal values — In this situation a person acts to accept a situation in life such as an illness.
> (pp.xvi,44,105)

Although the concept of meaning concerns the present, it also relates to the past. As Frankl (1985, p.118) notes "having been is still a mode of being." Therefore, the past activities of the older woman can be validated. Furthermore, the enduring nature of what has occurred previously confirms the importance of all activities covering a person's lifetime. Frankl (1985 p.120) eloquently illustrates that point when he states that the "wholeness of our life that is what we complete in the very moment of our death, lives outside the grave, it remains so not although but because it has slipped into the past."

A basic premise of Frankl's work is that individuals are free to shape their character and are responsible for what they make out of themselves. In a search for meaning in life and through their actions, they exercise freedom of will, an integral part of their humanness. Frankl provides a framework for focusing on how meaning is created through activity.

The following review is based upon a study of the aged population and older women in particular. The phenomenon of activity has been explored in the literature in relation to women and the aged population.

The Population

As the number of people over age 65 increases in the United States, concerns have surfaced about a population that will become more dependent and sicker. The advent of a greater focus on preventive health care however, offers promise of an improved future for persons in the elderly age group. Gallo, Reichel and Anderson (1995) note that increasing age brings many developmental challenges and that this may be a time of significant growth for many older individuals.

In 1991, there were over two million females compared to almost nine hundred thousand males over age 85 (U.S. Bureau of Census 1992). This disproportionate number is expected to continue as the gap in life expectancy persists. The average life expectancy of a male born in 1991 is 72 years as compared to 78.8 years for his female counterpart.

Other data show that approximately 40% of all individuals age 75 and over, live alone (U.S. Bureau of the Census 1992). In the aged population 85 and over 75% reside within the community, indicating that only about 25% require institutionalized care (AARP 1991). Of significance is that although the rate of increase of people over 85 has been dramatic, since the 1970s no marked rise has occurred in the percent of this group in nursing homes (Taeuber 1991). This finding may be due to no increase in the overall morbidity of this group. Another view suggested by Manton (1988) is that health care policy decisions by government agencies have led to constraints on the number of available nursing home beds as well as stricter admission policies.

Increasing age nonetheless can signal the probability of living in a nursing home, particularly for women. In 1985, 75% of nursing home residents were women age 85 and older (AARP 1991).

Functional limitations are a concern of the elderly population, and three of these have been identified in people 85 and over living in the community: (1) walking difficulty, (2) shopping, and (3) performing housework. Of interest is that only 38% of those with walking problems have received any help. Assistance is more likely to be available for shopping and housework (Taeuber 1991).

Although many of this age group show some degree of functional limitation, Longino (1988) noted that more than half of those non institutionalized, over age 85, considered themselves to be free of any problem in this area. In studying his sample in relation to mortality rates, dependency and need for resources, he observed that the latter variable may not be as great as anticipated. He considered it important to closely examine people of this age group in regard to health and financial needs.

The educational level of persons over age 65 is considerably higher in the 20-year span after 1970. Contemporary figures for the age group 85 and over reveal that more than half have completed only grade school, no significant difference between men and women (U.S. Bureau of Census 1992). It is projected that future groups of this age will be better educated in light of the higher educational level of those currently 65 and over.

In recent times, a major change for older women has been an increase in the probability of their living alone, particularly with increasing age. In 1991, 34% of females age 65 to 74 lived alone compared to 13% of males. In the age group 75 and over the figure climbed to 53% for females and 21% for males (U.S. Bureau of Census 1992). Thus, living conditions of older women vary considerably from those of older men.

Living alone can also be equated with poverty in older women. The American Association of Retired Persons (1991) found that people living alone or with non-relatives were more likely to be poor (25%) than those living with families (6%). AARP also noted that 40% of women 65 and older living alone were 25% below the poverty level. A related fact is that elderly women spent almost half of their income on housing.

In 1990 the median income for men 65 and older was $14,183 and $8,044 for women in the same age group. Furthermore, over 15% of women of this age group (2.7 million individuals) were living in poverty in 1990 as compared to less than eight percent of men 65 and older (959,000) (AARP 1991).

Marital status has a direct relationship to the living status of women. In 1990, 74% of men in the age group 85 and older were married and living with their wives, while only 40% of women in this group lived with their husbands (AARP 1991). Another finding was that older females were disproportionately dependent upon social security. Nine out of ten elderly unmarried (includes divorced, widowed and never married) women received social security benefits in 1988, with 20% having no other income. It can be concluded that although some individuals in the elderly population might have adequate income, considerably more women were apt to be poor.

In addition to the increased chance of being poor and living alone, women appeared to have more disabling conditions (such as arthritis), and therefore often reported higher rates of impairment than older men. On the other hand, men were more likely to have serious health problems, resulting in a greater risk of dying at any age (Herzog, in Herzog et al 1989).

Katz et al (1983) disputed the issue of women age 85 and over as being more disabled functionally than men. They studied the active lives of elderly men and women, using years of functional well being in relation to activities of daily living. Their findings consistently showed little difference in active life expectancy between men and women. At age 85, the average active life expectancy for both groups was 2.9 years. In their research, the investigators define active life expectancy as independence in the activities of daily living, as measured by a tool, the Index of ADL.

Women may become increasingly dependent as they reach the oldest age group, requiring more assistance with daily living. Haug and Folmer (1986) supported the finding that men who survived to the very elderly age group were comparable to women of the same age in performing activities of daily living. They suggest, however, that in situations of living alone, lower incomes, and health losses, the quality of life may be lower in women. Butler et al (1995) noted that gender bias continues to exist in health insurance and quality of treatment and creates special problems for the older woman who is likely to have several chronic diseases and no insurance coverage for prescription drugs.

In her study of health status and behaviors of a group of females age 85 and older, Oudt (1988) concluded that despite an average of two to three chronic illnesses, the subjects were generally independent, living alone and rated their health as good. Also, individuals with high health ratings were more apt to use self-initiated behaviors to stay well rather than health behaviors recommended by health care professionals. Only eight percent of the study population lived below the poverty level as compared to the national norm of 20%. This factor may explain their independence. Katz (1983) noted that active life expectancy was longer for the non-poor than for the poor.

Hoeffler (1987) examined marital status and its influence on the life outlook of the single older woman. She compared widowed, divorced, separated, and never married older women. Her study findings indicated that the never married group was better educated, healthier, less lonely, and had a more positive outlook than widowed women. No significant differences in these variables appeared between the divorced or separated women when compared to the never married. However, the divorced and separated group also perceived themselves as less healthy then their never married counterparts. The seemingly better life outlook of the never married group must be interpreted cautiously since three times the proportion of never married elderly women resided in institutions as compared with the numbers living in the community.

Health care has been a major expenditure in the United States, with 768 billion dollars spent in this area in 1992. Medicare costs accounted for approximately 128 billion dollars of total expenditures (Pear 1993). Although Medicare also provides funding for those persons permanently disabled, the bulk of this expenditure is spent on persons 62 and over. Rosenthal and Landefeld (1993) studied over 23,179 hospital admissions and found that the DRG adjusted charges were 6% higher for the age group age 85 and over compared with those aged 65 to 69. Government resources cover hospital and medical care but they do not provide for common items such as prescription drugs, hearing aids and preventive health examinations (Herzog in Herzog et al 1989). These items comprise a major expense for older people, particularly elderly women and markedly reduces their expendable income.

The aged population as a group face special challenges. Gallo, Reichel and Anderson (1995), note that the role of the elderly in other societies has often been more clearly defined than in our own. They are however optimistic that the elderly can be a valuable resource that needs to be drawn upon to share their knowledge.

GENDER, ECONOMICS AND ACTIVITY

Women and Gender

Few studies have focused on gender differences in the elderly, age 85 and over, but enough evidence exists in the number differences and income levels to document the need to do so. To date, there has been no consensus on what actually causes the gender differences between women and men although some studies point to hormonal influences, sociological, cultural and psychological factors (Ehrhardt, in Rossi 1985). Epstein (1989) stated that much of the problem stemmed not from the origins of the differences but how society interpreted them.

Their self development is an issue significant for women of all ages. Some theorists (Gilligan 1982), Surrey (1984) and Rossi (1985) have supported the importance of relationships in developing the self of the female. Surrey's view was that the self is organized and developed through practice resulting in mutually empathetic associations.

Since women at all ages seem to have a greater interest in maintaining relationships, the loss of peers and family in women 85 and older has become a serious issue when dealing with this age group. Belenky, Clinchy, Goldberger and Tarule (1986) studied a group of women from various rural and urban settings along with differences in educational background and income level. They examined women's ways of knowing, implying that their intellectual processes evolved differently. In this way, knowledge evolved from a passive stage of being voiceless and mindless to a position in which women experience themselves as a creator of knowledge.

Because women demonstrated different psychological strengths than men, they have often been thought of as weak or passive. According to Miller (1986) women more readily admit consciously to feelings of weakness or vulnerability. This awareness should place them in a position to understand weaknesses more easily in themselves as well as in others and, work productively to resolve problems. Exploring the supportive role of women, Miller noted they spent a large portion of their lives furthering the development of others. The supportive role of women becomes an important consideration when examining the meaning of the activities of women.

Women and Economics

The life activities of women age 85 and over have differed considerably from those of men in this age group, particularly in relation to work both within the home or workplace. The Industrial Revolution influenced the work roles of both men and women (Oakley 1974). During the 19th century, many of the goods and services produced by women in the home were increasingly being provided by a market economy (Blau 1978). Except for the time periods of World War I and World War II, most women were homemakers and economically dependent on men (Oakley 1974). After World War II, the high level of participation of women in the work force during the war did not continue. It was not until 1961 when the participation rates of women workers regained their 1945 levels (Blau 1978).

In 1930, the three top occupations in the numbers of employed women included domestic and personal service, clerical service, and manufacturing (Breckenridge 1972). Women who at present are 85 and over would have been at a prime career age at that time. Work opportunities were restricted to a narrow range of occupations. The State Education Department of New York conducted a study in 1993 on equal opportunity for women, in which it noted:

> Most women and men continue to be employed in traditional careers. Women are the majority of clerical and retail salesworkers, K-12 teachers and nurses. Men continue to hold the skilled labor jobs and dominate engineering, science and computer fields. Women have a disproportionate share of low paying jobs, are frequently overqualified for their work and do not get the same economic return on their education as men (1993, p.3).

The study affirmed the economic inequity between men and women, as well as the long delay in closing the gap. Even comparable education has not improved the situation. Women aged 25 and over with a four year college degree received 62 cents of each dollar earned by their male counterparts (The State Education Department 1993).

According to Epstein (1989), workplace boundaries exist and foster constraints related to gender. She pointed out that of all the boundaries acting as constraints, those defining gender work roles were the most persistent. Work associated with autonomy, prestige and authority was usually labeled men's work. Jobs considered non traditional to their sex continued to be labeled as men's even when women assumed them.

Since a woman's job is also viewed differently by society, its loss may not be considered as serious. This has been especially true for the older woman. Rodeheaver (1990) noted that older women face the same problems as older workers in general, but to a greater extent and earlier in the life course. They were also likely to have a longer job loss duration which means that once they lost a job, it was harder to find a new one.

A life time of working in the home without compensation or working in low paying jobs has resulted in reduced income for the elderly woman and an overdependence on social security.

Elderly females at various age ranges are less apt to have sufficient pensions and to be dependent on social security more than males (Kotilikoff 1983).

This problem, not unique to The United States, has been even more prevalent in undeveloped countries. In 1991, the United Nations stated the following in a report on women throughout the world:

> Governments do not consider much of women's work to be economically productive and thus do not count it. If women's unpaid work in subsistence agriculture, housework and family care were fully counted as productive outputs in labor force statistics, their share of the labor force would be equal to or greater than men's. And if their unpaid housework and family care were counted as productive outputs in national accounts, measures of global output would increase 25 to 30 percent. (United Nations 1991, p.2)

The activities of women have been devalued whether they occur in the home or in the workplace, (Epstein 1989; Folbre and Abel 1989). Feminist researchers such as Miller (1986) noted that many of the activities that women engaged in were viewed as passive, while those of men were considered active. She contended that most of the so called "women's work was not considered as real activity." (Miller p.52)

Oakley (1974) pointed out that the activities of housework, performed by the woman in marriage (the housewife), were omitted from employment statistics. Thus, a housewife was not considered employed. According to Folbre and Able (1989), the participation of women in the market economy, particularly before 1940, may have been seriously understated due to gender bias in census reporting. This same situation has persisted with women's unpaid work in the home not meeting the census definition of market work. Such a practice perpetuates the invisibility of women's contributions to society. The present study provides an opportunity for women to relate their past activities and discuss their work both inside and outside the home.

Activity

As mentioned earlier, major studies of activity in the older person have focused on functional ability and activities of daily living. The following review includes this area but also presents research that has examined variables such as choice, well being, life satisfaction, and health in relation to activity.

The concept of activity as movement or "doing" appears to be generally accepted. Beyond the basic interpretation, widespread diversity has arisen on what should be measured to determine human activity and how to do it. Also to be developed is a concept of activity from a feminist perspective. Since studies vary in their emphasis on activities, interpretation of the results must consider what the researcher has viewed as activity. Golant (1984) noted that few guidelines have existed to classify activities according to their purpose with such decisions often dictated by the goals of research.

Three major psychosocial theories have sought to explain activity in the aging person. Havighurst et al. (1968) proposed an activity theory which stated that the person who aged optimally was the one who stayed active and managed to resist the narrowing of his or her social world. Such people could maintain the activities of middle age as long as possible and then find substitutes for those to be relinquished. Cumming and Henry (1961) proposed their disengagement theory, which offered a contrasting view. They suggested aging as a mutual withdrawal of both society and the older individual. This response was thought to be necessary for successful adjustment in old age.

Havighurst and Neugarten (1968) studied the same group as in Cumming's and Henry's study, and proposed a third theory to explain activity in aging. They noted that disengagement was not supported nor did activity levels consistently explain successful adjustment in old age. Therefore, they developed a theory of continuity which considered the personality of the subjects and examined the behaviors over a period of time. Their results indicated that in normal men and women there was no sharp discontinuity of personality with age but an increasing consistency instead.

Essentially, Cumming's and Henry's subjects became more like themselves rather than less as they aged. This conclusion was supported by Maddox (1968), who examined the persistence of lifestyle among the elderly. He found that individuals who ranked high or low initially, tended to maintain this same activity level throughout. When disengagement was noted, it appeared to be more of a continuation of a particular lifestyle and not a process applicable to all aging individuals.

In a later work, Maddox (1991) observed that individuals aged differently and succeeded differently in aging well. His research also suggested that socioeconomic factors dramatically affected how a person ages. Although a lack of consistency has existed among theories of aging, there is support for a theory that allows for individual differences while explaining the aging process.

The focus on functional activities related to daily activities of the older individual has been justified as studies have demonstrated high correlations between nonperformance of ADL and health system use. Rubenstein et al. (1989) noted that deteriorations in functioning were common and often lethal manifestation of disease among elderly patients. Their research suggested using depression scales and mental status evaluations with a measurement of ADL to obtain a clearer picture of the person's health state. They did not explore how older people accomplished their activities of daily living or the relative importance of non performance.

Simonsick et al (1993) studied the impact of recreational physical activity upon functional status and mortality. Their findings suggested that physical activity offered benefits to physically capable older adults by reducing the risk of functional decline and mortality. Higher levels of recreational activity were noted to be associated with lower declines in functional ability over time. An important factor in the ability to perform functional activities has been noted in relation to performing manual tasks. In the Williams and Hadler (1982) study of dependency in women over 63 years of age, they determined manual ability to be the best indicator of dependency. The group consisted of institutionalized as well as non institutionalized subjects.

Aniansson et al (1980) studied functional capacity in the activities of daily living in 70-year old men and women. Their emphasis was on evaluating muscle strength, practical function tests, and activities of daily living thought necessary for independent living. Two significant findings in this Swedish study emerged: (1) Both sexes showed a decline in manual dexterity and (2) The mean walking speed was lower for both sexes.

Branch and Myers (1987) discussed assessing physical function in the elderly and noted that self report was a fairly reliable means to use, and possibly more reliable in regard to physical function than the use of an observer. Rodgers and Herzog (1987) suggested that information should be directly obtained from the elderly person. Their investigation compared the elderly with younger subjects in relation to accuracy of information. They found no consistent age differences in accuracy, but when some significant variation did occur, the older subjects were sometimes more accurate than the younger ones.

Health and function were studied by Ford et al (1988) who proposed that medically diagnosed diseases be separated from functional disability in assessing the aged. This research concluded that the detection of disease was necessary to define treatment needs, while function indicated what social support services were needed.

According to Cauley et al (1987), several different types of instruments should be used to measure physical activity. In studying physical activity in postmenopausal women, they did not find a significant relationship with risk factors such as bone loss. The results were thought to be related to the way in which the activity was assessed. In performing future studies the researcher indicated that the particular dimension of the activity being measured should be defined and more than one instrument used. Lawton's (1991) investigation of functional health and aging well suggested that in addition to assessing several dimensions of function, the researcher must include the way the person judged his or her own performance and in turn related this to their quality of life.

Gallo, Reichel and Anderson (1995) stress the point that specific functional loss in the elderly is not determined by the locus of disease. They suggest an awareness that medical and psychiatric illnesses may present as a nonspecific deterioration in functional status. Functional assessment can help the practitioner focus on the patient's capabilities and prevent small problems from becoming major disabilities.

Lombranz et al (1988) studied depression and well being in relation to indoor and outdoor activities. They compared both men and women and noted significant differences. The researchers observed that in elderly women the level or frequency of the activity in itself was a poor predictor of mood, whereas satisfaction derived from such activity was a good predictor. These findings indicated that the importance attributed to activity should be considered when predicting the mood of elderly people from their activity level.

Choice appears to be a significant variable to consider when examining activity in the elderly. Hulicka et al (1975) studied the perceived latitude of choice of institutionalized and non institutionalized elderly women. The results indicated that institutionalized women perceived themselves as having less choice; they also earned lower mean self concept and life satisfaction scores than the noninstitutionalized subjects. In general, the institutionalized group rated themselves less positively on all the descriptors related to self concept. The study supported the need to consider the institutionalized woman separately from the woman in the community and to consider choice in the examining of activities.

The variable of choice was also addressed by Cohen (1988), who investigated the limitations on the performance of social activity among a group of elderly with disabilities. He noted that there was a difference in the perceptions of disabled elderly and nondisabled elderly about their expectations as participants in society. Cohen further indicated that differences in expectations resulted in differences in how autonomy was applied.

Golant (1984) investigated activity in relation to the environment for a group of elderly living in Chicago. He found that the subjects were strongly linked to their outside social environment even without leaving their residence. They were connected through friends and family visiting as well as the use of mechanisms such as the telephone.

The study should stimulate further research that will include social activities occurring within the home as well as linkages to outside social ties.

Almind (1985) conducted an investigation of elderly persons age 80 and over in a Danish community. Although the study took place in a setting different from the health care system in the United States, it offered valuable data in examining risk factors for this age group living at home. The researcher was concerned with identifying factors that might predict future hospitalization and nursing home placement. Included were poor mobility, the need to take medication, poor memories, existing home nursing, and shortness of breath. An interesting observation was that at the end of two years, 75% of the 459 subjects still lived at home. Almind noted that in this community an adequate health care system was in place, and few changes were necessary to reduce the incidence of hospitalization and nursing home placement for high risk individuals.

Lawton and Fulcomer (1987) explored the relationship of time and activity. Their results indicated that the strongest determinant of time allocation was functional health, which appeared better among people spending time alone and outside the home in obligatory activities. This was thought to be related to impairments and declining health which may prevent the elderly from doing their own self maintenance activities. The investigators also noted that rest and relaxation activities increased as competency in daily activity decreased.

In research on activities in the elderly, leisure activities have been addressed separately from others, and often in relation to adjustment to retirement. Peppers (1976) studied the patterns of leisure and adjustment to retirement in a population of males with a mean age of 68. In considering both solitary and group activities, he noted that most of the more popular ones were isolated types such as reading and gardening. The same activities were also popular in the pre-retirement years. His results showed a higher life satisfaction score for those retirees in the sample who increased their level of activity as compared to those with constant or decreased activity levels. Activities, primarily social and or physical in nature, had the most positive effect on life satisfaction.

Gregory (1983) addressed the influence of meaning of activity on life satisfaction in retirees. He found that subjects scoring above the median on purposeful activity had significantly higher life satisfaction scores than those who did not. These findings supported the view that purposeful behavior played a significant role in affecting life satisfaction among the elderly. The study, which indicated a mean age of 75.4 years, did not identify the gender of the subjects and, therefore, no comparisons could be made between female and male subjects.

George and Clipp (1991) also discussed the relationship between life satisfaction and meaning. They suggested that the issue of life as having meaning be given a high priority for research. Although some older adults might find life unsatisfying, they nonetheless could discover meaning in it and in that sense age well. At the same time, the existence of life satisfaction and finding meaning in life did not necessarily imply that the two were synonymous or interdependent. Solomon and Peterson (1994) studied aging and suggested that the ability to view change as meaningful to one's life was an important key to successful aging. They further noted that being able to feel that one's life has a purpose enables an individual to endure great hardship.

Euler (1992) investigated life satisfaction in a group of subjects that ranged in age from 66 to 90. He observed that a weak relationship existed between superficial life satisfaction and deep psychological well being. His findings suggested that research on life satisfaction must move beyond such superficial indicators as income level and investigate sources of meaning in life of the elderly.

Tinsley et al. (1985) studied the psychological benefits of 18 commonly chosen leisure activities. His purpose was to develop a conceptual framework for understanding these benefits as derived from measuring the stated activities in subjects age 55 to 75. He developed a framework that grouped activities into clusters on the basis of their psychological benefits. Tinsley noted that clustering together might enable them to be substituted for each other since functional ability could interfere with the performance of some.

Summary of Literature Review

This literature review has focused on older women from the perspective of population and gender issues that may have influenced their lives. The research relating to the population of older women reveals different characteristics, when compared to that of older men.

While women may be more likely to live to the age of 85, they also tend to live alone and in poverty. Demographics about them have appeared in the literature but little is available about their activities. It has been suggested that the older woman is made to be "invisible." This remains true especially in health care where significant gaps continue to exist in the care of older women

Gender issues reported in investigations have ranged from role development to work opportunities. Although no consensus has been reached on the sources of gender differences, a sufficient number of studies seems to suggest that the life experiences of older women appear different from those of older men.

Activity studies have demonstrated well developed and useful tools on functional activities of daily living. They have shown significant correlations with important variables such as morbidity, mortality, institutionalization, and the individual's ability to live alone. Although they emphasize the empirical methodology and focus on functional performance they have not considered how the older person interprets the activity.

III

Gathering the Data

OBTAINING THE SAMPLE

The purpose of this study was to describe how women age 85 and over create meaning in their lives through activity. A qualitative methodology was selected, using grounded theory as a systematic process for collecting and analyzing data aimed to generate explanatory theory (Chenitz and Swanson 1986). The steps of grounded theory research occur simultaneously with the investigator observing, collecting data and organizing data, and forming theory. Two key points that distinguish grounded theory from other qualitative approaches include the use of a constant comparative method to analyze data, and the generating of the theory from that data (Glaser 1967; Darkenwald 1980). This method utilizes an inductive "from the ground up approach." The theory that develops from this type of research is grounded in the data from which it emerges and therefore becomes inherently relevant.

Study Population

The study population consisted of twenty women between the ages of 85 and 105. The women lived in private homes and public or private housing apartments in their respective communities.

The Setting

The population was selected from two suburban areas, one within New York City limits and one primarily residential, thirty miles north of the city limits. Both areas were predominately middle class. The one outside of city limits had a white population of 79% and a minority of 21%, while the one within the limits was 84% white and 16% minority.

Selection

The population was obtained from the directors of three senior centers as well as direct referrals from nursing professionals within the community

The Procedure

The researcher contacted the directors of several senior centers and received permission to approach potential female participants from their membership.

In the three centers, the director introduced the researcher to the women who met the inclusion criteria of the study. In the case of direct referrals from colleagues, the referral person first spoke with the women to obtain consent for the researcher to contact them. The researcher then followed up with a telephone call to schedule appointments.

Ethical Considerations

Participants were provided with a verbal explanation of the study, and then informed consent was obtained. Their participation was voluntary. The women were informed about their right to refuse to participate as well as to withdraw from the study at any time. They were assured that they could terminate the interviews whenever they chose to.

Sufficient time was allowed for the women to ask questions regarding the nature of the study. To assure their confidentiality and anonymity, their names were substituted by initials and then changed to further protect the individual's anonymity. A master list was used with the correct initials to allow the researcher to retrieve additional data if needed.

Consideration was also given to the comfort of the women, who were asked to notify the researcher at any time if they became physically or mentally uncomfortable during the interviews. The researcher was also sensitive to cues that indicated fatigue and would continue the interview at another time in case of this eventuality. This situation arose on two occasions

DATA COLLECTION

The Interview Process

Information pertaining to the research questions was obtained primarily through unstructured formal interviews and participant observation.

Although an interview guide was used, the researcher was free to interject other words and ask questions. Essentially, the unstructured interview would allow for more researcher and participant interaction without a rigid format to follow (Swanson, in Chenitz and Swanson 1986).

All the women were interviewed at least twice, with the first meeting designed to provide an introduction and establish rapport. In the case of women selected from the senior centers, the researcher met briefly with the individual at the center for the first time. An appointment was then made to conduct an interview in their homes. Participants referred by colleagues met briefly with the researcher in their homes for the first interview which was followed by a longer one. When the interview took place in the senior center, one of the offices not in use was provided to ensure privacy. Interviews conducted in the home were usually held in the kitchen or the living room. The researcher requested to see the woman alone when another person was present in the home.

Five of the twenty interviews were audiotaped; the remaining fifteen women did not wish to be audiotaped. In all cases, verbatim notes were recorded throughout the interview. During the process, some of the women would show the researcher around the home to point out certain objects or to go into the garden. In these instances, immediately after completing each interview, the researcher made additional notes regarding the participant's responses.

The initial interviews were from 15 minutes to an hour in duration. The second in-depth interview lasted a minimum of one hour. One of the women was interviewed three times at her request as she had "more to tell." The data were collected over a period of one year.

The Interview Guide

To focus the interview, a guide consisting of questions was used that aimed to elicit descriptions of the women's activities and explanations of their meaning. The responses of participants to some questions led to a rephrasing of them for others.

The initial questions were modified during data collection to reflect more closely the woman's language. For example, an initial question referred to *blocks* to activities. The participants, however, could not relate the term *blocks* to their own use of language. Thus, the question was modified to state: "What do you think stopped you from doing certain activities?" Also, any term that did not seem clear during the interviews was rephrased until an understanding of the terminology was reached between the woman and the researcher. The interview guide consisted of fourteen open-ended questions (Appendix B).

Participant Observation

Participant observation was used to supplement the data obtained from the interviews. The role of the participant observer can be viewed on a continuum. At one extreme is the observer who has minimal interaction with participants, while at the other end of the continuum, the researcher becomes completely involved (Bogden and Bilken 1983). In the present study, the researcher assumed a role approximately midway between these two points.

Participant observation consisted of informal talk and observing interactions. Informal talk between the researcher and the women occurred during the first contact either in the senior center or the home. These conversations focused on the weather, how the women were feeling, or what was happening that day at the center or at home.

The observation also consisted of watching the women's interactions in a group at the senior centers and in the homes whenever possible. The researcher engaged in such activities as sitting in a group during craft sessions at the center, sharing meals in the home, walking outdoors, and sitting in the garden.

The majority of the women were observed both inside and outside the home to provide a broader perspective. Chenitz and Swanson (1986) recommend this approach, noting that the meanings which objects, (people, values, articles etc.) hold for people cannot be divorced from the settings where they are experienced. It is vital to gain initially an understanding of activity by studying it in its natural setting: Observing the activities of older women both inside and outside the home provided this opportunity.

Field Notes

Field notes are a written account of what the researcher hears, sees, experiences, and thinks in the course of collecting and reflecting on the data in a qualitative study (Bogden and Bilken 1982). They may also contain a personal account of the researcher's experiences in the field. Field notes were made describing the physical setting of the individual's home. The investigator recorded detailed descriptions of objects such as furniture, pictures, and personal belongings. An example of such an entry is as follows:

> Pictures of people are noted on most of the available surfaces in the living room. Some of the pictures appear to have been taken recently while others seem to be from many years ago. The pictures are of people of various ages and are arranged in small collections.

Recordings were done on descriptions of the interactions of the women in groups and in their homes. The researcher also noted feelings that she experienced in the field. The recording of them helped to identify problems with the interactions. An example of this occurred with the first interview which did not seem productive. When the researcher reviewed the field notes describing her feelings during the interview, she discovered that a possible problem was that the woman's sister had remained in the room and occasionally interjected information. Thus, in subsequent interviews, the women were interviewed alone.

THE DATA

The data consisted of the women's responses during the interviews and field notes. Audiotaped interviews were transcribed verbatim, and all the interviews checked for completeness. If a response was unclear, the researcher asked the woman to validate the information. This situation occurred only twice. In one case, where the woman expressed ambivalence toward being alive, the researcher was uncertain if the analysis was correct. The participant was contacted and the interpretation validated.

The questions asked and the women's responses were placed in the left hand column of a transcript sheet. A right hand column was provided to allow ample room for the researcher to write her interpretations of the data. Field notes were placed on index cards and the interview they pertained to noted.

Data Analysis

Grounded theory methodology is distinguished from other qualitative methods in that data analysis begins with the generation of data (Glaser 1967; Darkenwald 1980).

After transcribing the data, the researcher began the coding process. Open coding, the specific method chosen for this study, is the analytic process whereby concepts are identified and developed in terms of their properties and dimensions. Strauss and Corbin (1991) describe three procedures that may be used for open coding. The first coding is a line by line analysis, the second by sentence or paragraph, and the third examining an entire document.

Data analysis for this study used the three procedures at different stages. At the outset, the researcher examined the entire document for a major theme, which was accomplished by asking at the end of each interview, "What seems to be going on here?". In one interview, for example, the researcher examined the document for a recurrent theme and found the idea of *loss* to be predominant throughout the process.

The second method of coding, which consisted of coding by paragraph was also used by the researcher initially. The following illustrates this approach:

> How do I feel about my life now. I get down some days
> thinking how no one comes by and how I can't do the
> ceramics anymore. But I guess I'm lucky I'm in my own
> home and I can still dress myself. I wish some old friends
> would stop by. We don't hear from them anymore.

In the above example, the woman referred to two major losses. Social losses were expressed as the loss of people coming into the house, and the loss of artistic creation in no longer being able to do ceramics.

While the use of analysis of paragraphs and the entire document generated basic concepts that would be validated throughout the data, these concepts could not be linked in such a way to build a theory. The researcher then began to analyze each interview with a line by line analysis by asking questions such as: "What activity is being carried out here?," "Under what conditions is it occurring?" and the basic question "What seems to be going on here?" The researcher closely examined phrases as well as single words.

An example of a line by line analysis is as follows:

> Q. Are there activities that you no longer engage in?
> A. There isn't too much I can do anymore. But it hasn't
> been that long that I've been like this. Maybe three years.
> Most days I can dress myself OK.

The participant sees herself with limitations but with some ability to function. She is able to recognize that she has not been limited long, and that there was a time she could do things. She sees the problem as recent and is able to place a time frame on the beginning of her losses which are temporal.

The process of line by line analysis was effective in producing information that could be used to build a theory. Theory building consists of first developing concepts or "conceptual labels placed on discrete happenings," regardless of the method of open coding (Strauss and Corbin 1991, p.61). In the present study, the concepts emerged as the researcher employed the actual words or actions of the participant and renamed them. One example was when most of the women used words such as "I can manage, I do all right, I can't do this but I'm still able to do. . . ." to describe their functioning. This concept was then labeled the *Able Self.*

An important part of data analysis is the making of comparisons. The researcher compared the concepts that were developing and categories or classifications of concepts began to emerge. This classification is discovered when concepts are compared against one another and appear to pertain to a similar phenomenon.

One of the categories that emerged was identified as *limiting losses*. It consisted of concepts such as friendship and independence. Comparisons were also possible by asking such questions as under what conditions does the limiting of losses occur. Specific activities were compared with others in the same category to establish if there was an appropriate fit.

The constant comparative method requires that not only data within the interview be examined for differences and similarities but also that developing categories be sought out in the next data set. Thus, once a specific category has been identified subsequent interviews are examined specifically to spot it again. To illustrate, early in the data collection the researcher noted the positive attitude of these women toward work.

Certain interview questions were then reworded to elicit more information concerning the women's experience of work. Essentially, the researcher asked the question: "If this women describes work in this way, how do others describe it?" The responses of each woman were always being compared to those that occurred previously.

After categories were identified, the next step of data analysis was to link the categories by posing questions about their relationships. Chenitz (1986) stated that the purpose of this procedure was to develop a final core category around which the theory may be built. Categories that evolved were linked together, and a final core category emerged that was grounded in the data.

Reliability and Validity

Reliability and validity have been sensitive issues in qualitative research. Reliability is the extent to which a measurement procedure yields the same answer however and whenever it is carried out (Kirk 1986). The inability to replicate in grounded research has been the major criticism of this method. Since the researcher is closely involved in the data analysis and contributes through close interaction in the field, no two analyses will be exactly alike. Chenitz and Swanson

(1986) noted, however, that when the grounded theory is developed, it should allow the researcher to interpret, understand, and predict phenomena in similar situations.

A valid study means that it measured what was intended by the researcher. In his discourse on validity in qualitative research, Maxwell (1992) reported that there was not only one correct objective account. He stated that as observers and interpreters of the world, people were inextricably part of it and could not step outside of their own experience to obtain some observer-independent account (of what they experienced). It was therefore possible to be valid in interpreting although it might differ from another's perspective.

In qualitative data, there must be concern that the propositions developed about the relationships are true (Glaser and Strauss 1967). The theory should fit with the data, which generate the appropriate categories. Therefore, the proof of the theory must lie within the data.

In order to increase the validity of the present study, the researcher used triangulation, a term derived from surveying. This involves taking a measurement from not just a single landmark but from two, with the surveyor located at their intersection (Fielding and Fielding 1987).

The basic procedure for triangulation is to check links between concepts and indicators by using other indicators. The form used in this study was data source triangulation. In this method, data related to the same phenomenon were compared but from different sources. Field notes obtained from participant observation were compared for similarities with the data from the interview responses. They contained information that resulted from speaking to others who knew the women as well as direct observation of the activities of the women. Hammersley and Atkinson (1983) supported the use of this form of triangulation, employing both participant observation and interview, to increase the validity of the study.

The comparison of data against data also served to increase the validity of the study. The researcher asked questions of how the data fitted the emerging categories. Data that were inappropriate were discarded. Maxwell (1992) noted that qualitative studies were usually not designed to allow systematic generalizations to some wider population. The external validity and the ability to generalize the results of the study to other populations become limited when the population has been confined to a particular age group, gender, or social class. The population for this study was sought with a purposeful selection of gender and age. The research aimed to develop a theory that would explain a basic social process for a select group of women. It is hoped that the theory which emerged may be studied with other populations to increase the external validity.

IV

Making Do

THE DEMOGRAPHICS

Twenty women shared their life experiences for this study. They ranged in age from 85 to 105 with a mean age of 89.7 years. Seventy percent lived alone, a figure higher than the national average of 53% for women over age 75 (U.S. Bureau of Census 1992). This observation may reflect the fact that the U.S. Census Bureau only records data on living arrangements as over age 75 and not over age 85. Also important is that the chances of a woman living alone increase with age. In the sample, 14 participants lived alone, one lived with a spouse, and five lived with other family members.

Sixteen of the twenty women were widowed. One was single while four of the women had been divorced and two of these who later remarried were subsequently widowed. Only one woman lived with a spouse. In this age group, women were far more likely to be widowed and less apt to remarry than older men (Holden, in Herzog et al 1989).

Twenty-five percent of the study population received a pension while the remaining depended on social security for income. At the national level only 21% of women age 65 and over had any type of pension income in 1990, according to their own or their husband's employment record (AARP 1991).

The lack of a pension for three fourths of the participants resulted in a number of them living marginally on social security alone. This lack of coverage can be attributed to several factors, none the least being that retirement plans did not begin until after World War II. Holden (1989) noted that pension coverage for all workers was related to firm size, union status, education of the workers and earnings. Another factor was that women were less likely to be employed in manufacturing and unionized industries, in which the awarding of pensions was high. While several of the women in the present study had been employed in unionized industries, most did not work in those settings. Furthermore, the interrupted work history of many due to child care undoubtedly negated against any type of pension coverage.

Most of the fourteen women who lived alone resided in either affordable rent-controlled or subsidized housing and, therefore, were able to meet their living expenses. Their ability to function and live alone was important to them. Only two of the five women who lived with family members indicated that they preferred this arrangement. The other three noted that if they could manage physically and financially, they would rather live alone.

The overall mean years of education for this group was nine and a half years. All the participants had at least an eighth grade education, with two of the women completing high school and one a diploma nursing program. In general, their educational level was comparable to that of the national average (U.S. Census 1992).

In 1955, labor force participation was approximately 43.8% among women 45 to 54 years of age (Holden in Herzog et al 1989). Most of the women in this study would have been within that age group at the time.

When asked to describe their activities outside the home, many related long work histories. Eighty percent (16) of the participants had been engaged in work other than the care of a home and family during their adult life. For three of these working women, the job consisted of piece work involving dressmaking and sewing alterations that were done at home or in small local businesses. The remaining thirteen were employed for long periods throughout their lives in such occupations as bookkeeper, clerk, nurse, and utility worker. The study sample appears to have had a greater work force participation than the norm for this age group. The nature of their occupations, however, would seem to reflect the restricted employment opportunities for women of their times.

THE RESULTS

Addressing the Research Questions

The core research question to be addressed in this study was: How do the activities of older women help them create meaning in their lives? Within this context were two other research questions as follows: (1) How do women age 85 and over define activity? and (2) What were the activities of these women?

In seeking responses to the first question, the investigator asked each participant to define activity in her own words. Some women had difficulty with the term and were better able to define it as "to be active." All were able to discuss activity and relate it to their own lives. Themes of energy, getting around, experiencing and personal choice emerged. One woman's description suggested that of energy:

> Activity is getting around real good — to have that push to
> do it

Another woman indicated choice as part of being active:

> Activity means to be doing something — can do it alone or
> do what you want. I'm active when I want to be.

Still another participant perceived being active as having dimensions other than physical.

> To be active means to be alert. They say about me: "Look
> at G.F. she doesn't look 88. Look at how active she is." To
> have your mind. I forget sometimes but I still have my
> mind.

One 89 year old woman simply answered:

> Activity is doing things

A 92-year old woman viewed activity as something she chooses to do and not what was necessary for daily living.

> Activity to me means doing something like
> my sewing that I showed you. Playing cards on Thursday
> night. That too.

At age 105, the oldest study participant noted:

> Being active. I guess it's getting around. I guess just what I
> do every day is activity. You just keep going. It's part of
> being alive.

Overall, the women defined activity in a personal way, relating it to their own lives at the present time. The definitions ranged from basic activities of daily living to mental processes. All the participants seemed to imply energy but not necessarily of a physical nature. They were able to relate some activity that they engaged in. The concept of activity appeared to have mental and social dimensions as well as the basic activities of daily living. As one participant above noted: "It's part of being alive." This interpretation is consistent with Frankl's (1985) view that the individual responds by action to life.

Although many of the study participants indicated the activities that they had difficulty with, no one described herself as not engaging in any or being inactive. Commonalties appeared in the responses but each woman interpreted activity differently and from her own perspective. The reaction was intensely personal and the concept of activity represented a life process.

The second research question aimed to address the nature of the activities that the twenty participants chose to engage in on a regular basis. Their responses showed the activities to be those that fostered a sense of connectedness and independence. These two categories became evident early on in the study and their manifestations appeared consistently throughout each interview.

Connectedness

Superficial Connecting. Connecting with others whether within the family or from social interaction outside the home seemed to be a driving force for most of these women. The first subcategory under connecting deals with outside social activities. It was named *superficial connecting* because of the observed social interactions. There appeared to be a desire to be part of the group, although few deep relationships were formed. The major goal was the interaction with others.

The two types of activities noted in this category were described as *cooperative and parallel.* Cooperative activities would include only those women who attended a senior center or community group regularly, and were sufficiently mobile to move about. Such activities also consisted of lunch preparation, planning for group outings, and participating in or organizing a group event like a musical show.

One participant described her church activities that included modeling for fund raising shows. Another participant led the researcher about a senior center while describing the craft group she helped to organize.

> We made the dolls last year. We kept some for show. I thought making dolls was something nice we could do for the children. The director gave us the material and I got everyone together.

Parallel activities were those in which the participants engaged in a *side by side* activity with minimal one-to-one interaction. An example of parallel activity observed was engaging in the game Bingo. In the present study, parallel activities were found to be more prevalent among participants with limited mobility. For some of the women, their primary reason for attending the center or other community activity was to be "among the people" rather than any specific one-to-one interaction.

Mrs. G.F. related the following in regard to her daily attendance at the center:

> My days would be dead if I didn't come here. Been coming here 16 years. I come every day. I come to talk to people. I guess I come to keep going.

Another participant, Mrs. A.H., also spoke of the importance of talking to people.

> I try to keep busy everyday. It's hard. My old friends all moved away or are dead. But I go to the center. I talk to people. I have my job there.

Mrs. B.J. clearly articulated her reason for coming to the center:

> It helps to talk to people. I come out to socialize. I go on trips. I come out as much as I can. I feel good when I talk to people.

Mrs. G.F. also spoke of overcoming difficulties just to be with others:

> I come here every day even in the winter. I stand out in the
> cold to wait for the bus to come here. It isn't good to be
> alone. That's why I do it.

One participant, Mrs. B.J., identified her feeling about socializing:

> The most important thing I do now is getting out. You
> have to mix in with people.

For some participants, the amount of socializing they experienced was inadequate. One participant related the following when asked what activities were the most difficult to give up:

> Going out to restaurants. I used to like nice seafood
> restaurants down the Jersey Shore. We went out, we did
> things like that. Now, I'm a shut in. I had to give up going
> out because I couldn't walk.

Mrs. O.L. explained that socializing at the center did not involve friendship but it was important to her:

> The most important part of my day is here. I see people who come over.
> I talk. I can't walk around but they talk to me. I never had a lot of friends
> except in Italy. I come here to see the people. Better than sitting in my
> place.

Leaving the house to be among people was not something one 89-year old woman was able to do. Unable to socialize outside her home, she spent time alone anticipating the visits of people:

> There are no friends that come around anymore. That's
> just how it is when you get old and you spend a lot of time
> alone. Right now, I just look forward to the days, when I
> have company.

Mrs. G.D. who lives alone and "kind of likes it that way," pointed out how important people were to her:

> I like to have something to do. I go out if I have a place to
> go to. I like a lot of people.

Connecting with others was an important activity for these women. In their disengagement theory, Cumming and Henry (1961) described aging as a mutual withdrawal of both society and the aging individual, which they thought was necessary for successful adjustment in old age. Yet, the lives and words of the women in the present study did not support a disengagement theory. Rather, a concerted effort was seen to maintain social contacts even when it was physically difficult to do so. The activities of these women appeared more congruent with the view of Maddox (1991), who stated that there were many differences in how people aged successfully. He attributed the variations to how social and economic resources were allocated over the life span as well as socioculturally defined expectations about the meaning of being older.

A commonality among these women was the difference in the type of social connecting that they engaged in at present as compared with earlier social relationships. Being with people and getting out among them seemed to be the major form of social connecting. Many of the participants spoke of the loss of friends even though they socialized on a regular basis with others. One woman Mrs. G.D. who was 86 years old spoke of missing friendship in her life:

> I'm here by myself. My friends are dead. I had a friend here. We were close but we aren't anymore. I had a very good friend. I sure miss her. She is dead about ten years now.

Mrs. T.E. differentiated between her friends at the center and friendships from earlier years:

> Thirty-four years ago we opened the center. I have a nice time here but my friends are all dead. I had a good friend. We did everything together, then she died. I have friends here but it isn't like an old friend.

These women consistently spoke of being with people at the center but did not refer to them within the context of a friendship. In their study of friendship in later life, Roberto and Kimboko (1989) noted that older women rather than older men were more likely to consider friends made earlier in their lives as still part of their network. The major reason given by study participants for the loss of friendships was death. It appeared that long-term relationships endured until death severed them.

In contrast to Roberto and Kimboko's work, in which 94% of the participants reported having at least one close friend, the women in the present study repeatedly stated that they had no friends. The difference could be attributed to the mean age of 71.6 in the Roberto and Kimboko's study as compared with 89.7 years in this research. It could be concluded that the longer a person lived, the greater the chance that their close friendships would diminish.

Kaufman (1986) noted from her study on older persons that age affected friendship patterns in two ways:

> Quite a few people mention the fact that they have outlived many or most of their friends and this saddens them greatly. All of those who discuss friendship state that one does not make close friends when one is old. They feel that friendships depend upon building a life together, looking forward to the future and sharing expectations (p.110).

This explanation may account for the lack of "real" friends among the study participants. As old friends died, the type of social connecting that was occurring assumed a more superficial form. As a result, there was a limited sharing of activities such as Bingo, or just sitting with others in a group. To the study participants a friend meant being together over a long period of time, nevertheless, the women apparently believed that they were achieving a benefit from being with other people and interacting.

As G.F. noted:

> My days would be dead if I didn't come here. It isn't good to be alone. That's why I do it.

Although this level of social interaction did not seem to replace long-term friendships, it provided a means for connecting. In cases where the women did not actively participate in a group, the act of being present seemed to generate a sense of belonging.

Only two of the twenty participants, who did not leave the house regularly, did not seem to desire more social connecting than what they were experiencing. One participant, Mrs. M.R., had many family members who visited on a regular basis and had never been active in activities outside the home. The other, Mrs. P.M., had spent her life focusing on her daughter and late husband. Although, she once belonged to a choir, she relinquished this activity when her husband retired thirty years earlier. In her present situation as an older woman, she appeared unable to enter new social situations even if her daughter was willing to provide transportation.

Hesitant Outsider. This was the second subcategory related to a type of connecting that occurred within the family unit. Of the twenty participants, there was only one without any family members who provided social contact. Because of distance, several participants maintained communication through letters and telephone calls. Even when the women lived within a family unit, however, they were reluctant to seek out and connect with family members. The following illustrates the behavior of the hesitant outsider.

Mrs. T.E., a 91-year old woman who lives in an apartment in her son's house, described her relationship with the family:

> I cook my own food. I eat alone. I wish my daughter in law would be more friendly but I guess its better, I keep to myself. I wish she would talk to me more but I don't ask. I don't want to be a bother. I cook for myself. They eat young people's food. I eat old lady's food.

The participant saw herself as separate from the family even in relation to her food which she cooked and ate alone. Although desiring more connecting, she was unable to ask. A similar hesitancy occurred with Mrs. M.I:

> The hardest thing to give up was going out. I need someone to take me. I can't do it alone. I used to go to Bingo twice a week. They should know I would like to go. I would like them to say they would do it. If people don't offer, they don't want to do it. I don't like to ask them to do things for me.

Mrs. M.I. explained her situation further:

> My friends are all dead and my other daughter died too.
> The daughter that lives here works all day in the City, and
> when she comes home she is busy. I don't like to interfere
> but I wish we could do more things together. I try to stay
> out of their way even though this is my house.

Mrs. L.C. who is 94 years old expressed her feelings:

> My daughter comes by sometimes with groceries. I have a
> friend who gets me some too. I don't ask my daughter for
> too much. She has her own things to do but she helps out
> with the rent.

Another woman, Mrs. G.D., stated that it could be difficult to connect
with one's family and sometimes she felt that the activity was too
much for her:

> I like movies but I would be afraid to go out at night. If it
> was safer, I would go once in a while. I've been taken but
> it's hard to connect with the family and I don't like to ask.

She elaborated:

> Sometimes maybe its my age. The kids running around. I
> guess I'm old but I don't feel different.

Mrs. G.D. believed that the problems she encountered with her
family were related to age differences. Her aging status was difficult
for her to accept because she did not feel old.

Many subjects in Kaufman's (1986) research on older persons
expressed the same feeling. The investigator found that although her
subjects did not deny being old, they had not defined themselves in
this way.

Kart (1990) noted that there has been a transformation of the
extended family into a nuclear family in industrialized societies:

> Advocates of this view argue that extended families are
> advantageous in agrarian societies because all family
> members (including children and the elderly) contribute
> economically to the family. This is not the case in an
> industrial society, however, where children and the elderly

are largely unemployable. Moreover, because they consume at a high rate, these dependent relatives are a burden rather than an advantage. (p.219)

Krout's (1988) work with individuals age 65 and over revealed that the frequency of visits to older parents by adult children was mainly related to proximity. In the present study, visits at least several times a week were the norm for the study participants who had children living nearby. Some of the women admitted how much it meant to them when their adult child came home. The following comments of two participants illustrated this:

From Mrs. R.K., a 92 year old woman who was alone during the day:

The best time of the day is when my daughter comes home. I fix her dinner and we eat together, the cooking is about all I can do around here.

From Mrs. B.J. age 85:

You have to mix in with people. Most of my friends are dead. The best part of my day is when my daughter comes home. We have dinner together. I bake still. I make things she likes. My other daughter lives in Florida but this daughter takes care of everything.

Although these women seemed to express satisfaction with family relationships, many desired more interaction. At the same time, there was a reluctance to ask for assistance with an activity not considered a necessary, such as going to Bingo.

One explanation for this behavior could be the older person's reluctance to verbalize her needs. There also was the fear of being a burden because of the assistance needed to carry out activities of daily living. This feeling of not wanting to be a burden was consistently verbalized by the participants.

In their research on social support exchanges between persons 75 and over and their support networks, Ingersoll-Dayton and Talbot (1992) found that many of the subjects were able to draw on their past contributions and did not consider themselves a burden. This ability to recognize previous contributions made to the family may assist the older person to ask for assistance without hesitancy.

The study participants appeared to have different expectations of family members than of other persons with whom they connected. Their reluctance to verbalize their need for interaction, coupled with increased needs, seemed to result in a connecting pattern within the family that was unsatisfactory for many of them.

Independence

The second major category consisted of activities that produced a sense of independence. Within this grouping were three subcategories, described as relinquished activities, marginal activities, and adequate activities.

Relinquished Activities. Relinquished activities included those that are no longer performed, either due to physical limitations or the absence of opportunities. Discussion with these women regarding activities engaged in throughout their lives revealed the importance of work to them outside the home. Most (80%) had been employed for long periods throughout their lives. This activity was described as relinquished since only two of the women continued with outside work which was limited to about ten hours a week

Work appeared to be valuable to them in light of the social connections it provided as well as fostering a sense of self worth. Although some women had relinquished this activity many years earlier, they frequently verbalized that they missed it and would work at present if they could.

The following participants shared their perceptions of the work activity in earlier years. One 92-year old woman began to work full time when she became a widow:

> I had my daughter. I sent her to college. I worked sewing
> 24 years and liked it. I did good work.

Another woman spoke with pride of her years of bookkeeping.

> I was always good with numbers. There were three adults
> in the house. They only had to watch the children when
> they came home from school. So, I took a test and got a
> job. I was very good at it.

Mrs. O.L., who was 87-years old, noted that given a choice she would still be working.

> I was a Wall Street clerk and then worked for the state. I worked 'til I was 70. They made me retire. I would have kept working if I could.

Mrs. B.J. spoke of her feelings about work:

> When I got married, I worked at sewing for five years. Then I had one child. My sister in law took care of the children. I worked for General Electric and did it all. I liked work. It was hard. Not so different now is it? You do what you have to. I needed to work but I loved it.

Later, this same woman commented on one aspect of the work that she missed.

> You know I still miss work seeing the faces and talking to the people.

Mrs. M.I. is an 88-year old woman with a long work history at a utility company. She returned to her job when the children were small because her husband was ill.

> I would take care of the kids before I went to work and the house and my husband. Then he died and my mother came to live with me to help out. Her sight was real bad by then and I would worry about her at the stove at night. I worked from 4:00 p.m. to 12:00 p.m. I was a supervisor by then but I had to give it up so I could work when the kids were in school. If anything happened, I would have never forgiven myself. I had no choice but it was hard to give up because I liked being in charge and I did a good job.

Two of the women continued to do outside work. Ms. A.H., 85-years old, is employed at the senior center two days a week. She takes two buses to reach the center, often waiting a long time. This participant clearly separates her days of work from other days at the center. She stated that she will not change centers because her work is there, and described her activities as follows:

> I work there in the kitchen two days a week. The other
> days I just go to be with the people. I worked in a state
> school for twenty years mending clothes. They made me
> retire. I would have worked longer. I could still you know.

Another 89-year old woman, Mrs. A.B. verbalized how much her work meant to her and how she resented giving it up:

> I had a child, my son at 25, but I kept on working. I had
> worked on the PT boats, building them, and then I went to
> work for a department store. First, I was just a sales girl
> and then I was in charge of the stock room. I had friends
> there I always did a good job. I was fair to the girls. I loved
> the work.

She later described how her husband didn't want her to work because they had enough money.

> He made me quit, but I never wanted to. I started going
> out during the day to lunch with the ladies from the
> neighborhood, but I never liked that much. I loved my job.

Work for most of these women was necessary work in that they did so to support their families or themselves. The same situation applies to the working woman today. Only for the privileged class has there been an economic choice of whether to work. The fact is that women have always worked, but what has changed over time has been the relationship between paid labor and volunteer efforts.

The participants' work history paralleled time periods of major social and economic turmoil in America. During the Great Depression in the 1930s men and women found limited opportunities. The advent of World War II, however, increased the employment of women as men vacated jobs to join the armed services. Most of the older women in the study population continued to work after the War, engaged mainly in occupations considered to be traditionally female at that time.

Of interest is that some of the women were employed in work considered to be menial, and yet they spoke of "loving it." In contrast,

Simone de Beauvoir (1991) described the work of women within the home as follows:

> Thus woman's work within the home gives her no autonomy; it is not directly useful to society, it does not open out on the future, it produces nothing. It tries on meaning and dignity only as it is linked with existent beings who reach out beyond themselves, transcend themselves, toward society in production and action. . . . However respected she may be, she is subordinate, secondary, parasitic. . . . (p.349)

This observation may help to explain the meaning of work to these women. Unquestionably, salaried jobs performed outside the home provided them with a positive sense of self. They saw themselves as doing "good work." This self perception, however, may be based more on society's interpretation of work within the home rather than the actual paid work performed. Housework has been considered invisible as well as unpaid. Vanek (1978) related the following:

> Does housekeeping have productive value? It is not figured on national accounting systems and does not receive monetary rewards. Since no price is put on housework, people overlook its value. (p.393)

The work of women in the home remains as uncounted labor. A study conducted by the United Nations (1991) concluded that if women's unpaid housework and family care were viewed as productive outputs in national accounts, measures of global output would increase from 25% to 30 %.

Throughout their working lives, study participants encountered discrimination. They did not receive comparable pay commensurate with their job. Yet, the fact that the work was paid labor may have contributed toward their sense of self worth.

Among the relinquished activities, those presenting the greatest difficulty for these older women concerned required transportation assistance. Only one study participant was still driving a car whereas the others had to depend on family members for transportation. One center, however, provided this service.

All the women needed help with food shopping. Even the one participant who drove was accompanied by a neighbor who carried the

packages. Several women were able to continue shopping if they had
an assisting person, but many had to relinquish this activity. In such
cases groceries and supplies were brought into the home. A participant
described how much she missed this activity.

> It's just not the same. You make a list for them, but you
> can't pick things without seeing them. Sometimes, just
> looking myself would be good but I can't.

Another women indicated what she would consider to be a
perfect day:

> Going shopping for clothes and for things for the house to
> be able to see things before you buy them. Not like I have
> to do in getting things through the mail. Then, I'd like to
> go for a nice dinner and a show. But I can't with this
> wheelchair.

Other relinquished activities involved leaving the home solely for
social activities. Several of the women gave them up because of
physical disabilities. Major difficulties occurred primarily with
walking and standing. Urinary incontinence also presented a problem
for several of the women, and for one it was compounded by fecal
incontinence.

> I used to do ceramics at the center but I haven't been able
> to go there for about three years. I was hardly going when
> the bowel problem started, but I would go once in a while
> if I was having a good day. Then the last time I went, I had
> an accident. I was so embarrassed that I never went back.

In this older woman's situation, the loss of control over bodily
function led to a loss of doing ceramics. Relinquished activities were
often explained in comparison with activities still performed. One
participant noted giving up using public transportation and heavy
housework, while still performing self care.

> I gave up things. Sure I can't do them anymore. The
> windows, the bus, I never went too far but I can't go

anyplace anymore. The steps, I can't do them. My hands lock. The arthritis can't sew but I take care of myself. I can shower. I can wash my clothes.

Relinquishing an activity can be related to a lack of opportunity. In one situation, the participant no longer did some activities because they were performed by the family.

I don't cook anymore. The buttons on the stove are hard but I can see them. Maybe I could cook if I had to but I don't. I live here with my daughter and her husband, but it's my house. I can't bend too good and I can't kneel. I can sweep but they take care of that too. There isn't too much I have to do.

Heavy housework represented another relinquished activity but none of the women indicated that it was difficult to give up. About half of them used paid cleaning persons, whereas adult children assisted the other women.

In relation to activities no longer performed, the study findings were similar to those of a National Health Survey which identified three major functional limitations for the population, age 85 and over. Included were walking, shopping, and doing heavy housework (Taueber 1991). The survey pinpointed shopping and heavy housework as activities with which the older persons received help. Although people were limited in walking, most of them did not have assistance in this activity on a daily basis. Except for one woman, the participants in the present study were able to walk independently with assistive devices in the home.

In describing the activities of older women, it is important to consider why certain activities are no longer performed. The category of relinquished activities has revealed physical decline to be strongly related to giving them up. At the same time, many activities could be continued with minimal assistance, such as the availability transportation.

Marginal Activities. The subcategory of marginal activities involved those which these women performed, but with great difficulty or partial assistance.

Food preparation was a problem for many of the participants. Contributing factors included the inability to stand at the stove as well as poor vision to see the stove controls. One woman explained:

> I get two meals here (at the center). I can't cook too much anymore but I do a little like heating food. My daughter brings food over.

Another woman managed food preparation along with rest periods:

> First, I get everything out. Try to keep it plain. Just some meat and a vegetable. I rest, then I cook. Things I can leave on the stove work best.

Walking is an activity that presents a problem for most persons over age 85, and the participants in this study proved to be no exception. One person was confined to a wheelchair for most of the day. Only four women did not use any assistive devices for walking such as canes or walkers. One woman described her difficulty walking and the barriers she encountered:

> I can't get around too good. I have to use this walker. It's so clumsy, hard to get through doors.

Another woman noted that although she used a walker she could attend the center because it was barrier free. She was unable to attend church, however.

> I take the elevator. Its OK. No steps. The weekends I watch mass on television. I can't go anymore. Two blocks are too hard. I went 'til two years ago. I can't do it.

Walking within the home environment was possible for Mrs. N. with the use of a walker, but outside walking presented a problem:

> About five years, I guess I've been like this. I need this walker. Get dizzy, have to be careful. I can't shop or take a bus or go out myself.

For these women, the major reasons for difficulty in walking were arthritis, cardiac conditions, and equilibrium imbalance. Among older persons, chronic illness has become common. Arthritis is one of the more prevalent health problems of older women, more so than of men. Herzog (1989) observed that arthritis was one of the most painful and disabling chronic conditions. Also, the accompanying pain, stiffness, and joint swelling affected the ability of the afflicted person to walk and perform other activities.

Equilibrium imbalance, a problem frequently related to degenerative changes in the nervous system, results in symptoms such as dizziness, loss of balance, and falling. The vestibular system, which provides a sense of balance and spatial orientation, degenerates in older persons (Thomas 1992).

In addition, there is a degeneration of kinesthesis, or the ability to sense various parts of the body and movement of the limbs, also degenerates. These changes create the difficulties for older women who complain of dizziness while walking, falling backward, and inability to climb stairs.

Hypertension affects up to fifty percent of the population by age 80 (Burdman 1986). It weakens the heart and increases the risk of heart attack and stroke. In the older person, cardiac output is reduced, resulting in decreased perfusion of body tissues. The heart's ability to pump blood lessens with age. A thickening of the left ventricular wall occurs as well as a thickening of the valves. These changes contribute to activity intolerance. Several of the study participants experienced chest pain while walking whereas others cited fatigue and a need to rest.

Adequate Activities. The subcategory labeled as adequate involved activities which most of the women were able to perform with no assistance. Included were basic activities of bathing, dressing, and light housekeeping. Two participants required some help with bathing but were independent in dressing. They also could not perform light housekeeping. One woman resided with her husband who assisted her, whereas the other had a home care aide for twelve hours a day. Based on their own self report, the remaining eighteen women were assessed as performing these activities at an adequate level.

One 92-year old participant used a walker and was unable to do heavy housework or shopping. She articulated what she could manage in her environment:

> I can heat my food. I wash every day. I wash my clothes.
> I'm careful. Sometimes I lose my urine so I wash. I fix my
> hair. I wipe the table off. I wash the floor. I use the
> vacuum but I can't move too much. I have to rest after.

The importance of dressing oneself was related by Mrs. A.B. who
needed some assistance with bathing:

> He helps me out (of the shower). Then I get dressed. It
> takes a long time some days. I have to go slow. I feel good
> if I can just get myself dressed. You feel like a baby if
> someone dresses you.

Although this older woman had many functional limitations, the
act of dressing herself represented a degree of independence and
maintaining her identity as an adult.

Another activity, in which all twenty participants were judged as
functioning adequately, was their mental processes. They were able to
make correct decisions on a daily basis to maintain a safe environment
for themselves. Although some complained of forgetfulness, their
memory was sufficient so that they remembered to eat, take their
medications, and perform basic activities such as washing and
dressing. This assessment was based mainly on their self report and
verification, whenever possible, by others known to these women.

Many participants verbalized mental functioning as the most
important activity to retain. One woman who was 94 years old said she
didn't worry about things until something happened; but the loss of her
mental processes would concern her. To her, it would represent her
life being over.

> I just hope the mind is good. If the mind crumbles, then its
> over.

The present study was limited to women who were aware of who
they were and oriented to the month and the place. Therefore, the fact
that mental processes were retained for this group was an expected
finding. Through their words, the women suggested that the loss of
functional abilities could be dealt with and a degree of independence
retained. The loss of their mental processes, however, would result in a
loss of self.

The activities that these women could perform at an adequate level were critical to avoiding institutionalization. Major functional disabilities, particularly feeding, urine control, and mental disorders all contributed to the likelihood of being institutionalized (Herzog 1989). Despite major difficulties with some activities and a predominate need for assistive walking devices, these women were able to use community and family resources to remain within their homes.

In this investigation, the first two research questions in this study were largely descriptive in nature whereas the third research question represented the core of the study and asked: "How do the activities of these women help them create meaning in their lives?" Becker (1993) noted that the goal of grounded theory research was discovery. She compared the descriptive mode of research with the discovery mode:

> Although the two appear very similar, the goals are different. In the descriptive mode, description is an end in itself. It serves to answer the question, "What is going on here?" In the discovery mode, descriptions means to an end. The end is to answer the questions "What is going on and how?" (p.255)

The "what" has been addressed. The "how" explains the process through which these women created meaning in their lives through activity.

The Core Category: The Making Do

Making Do, the core category, was named by analyzing the words used by participants to describe how they were living their lives at that time as well as past life experiences.

Mrs. L.C. described how her daily life was at present:

> I live with my daughter now and her husband but I try to take care of myself the best I can. I do my own cleaning. I sew a little. I get up about 6:00 a.m. I just wake up. It takes me awhile to get going. I make my own breakfast. I tidy up a little. I need help with the vacuuming. Otherwise, I can manage. If I get tired, I just lay down.

She further related how she felt about her life:

> I feel pretty good. I am satisfied. I love everything I did. I
> love my life the way it is.

The woman came from a wealthy family and then adjusted to a
marriage with a man of lesser means.

> My father was very generous. He owned two meat
> markets. He was a good provider, but when I married I
> said what we don't have I'll go to work for. I'll make my
> own. Work was something I looked forward to. I'm fine.
> I'm 94. I make the best of everything. Don't worry 'til
> something happens.

Another participant, Mrs. M.R. related how she was managing at the
present time.

> Things now? How is it? It's all right. Not so hard anymore.
> People they complain. I say you be grateful. During the
> war, there wasn't much food. We had animals, we grew
> vegetables, we give some away. We helped others.

 She further described a sense of satisfaction with her life and what she
was able to accomplish:

> I feel happy. Not afraid. I don't do anything bad. I take
> good care of the kids. The morning is good. I have
> strength. I go to the garden. I dig. I plant. In the winter, I
> work in the house. I fix the bread. The kids come by, I
> make them food. I go slow. I like all my life.

Mrs. T.E. who was 91, married at twenty years of age. Although
somewhat hindered by a domineering husband, she managed to
contribute to the support of the family. She recounted this situation as
to how she was able to care for herself at present:

> My husband never let me work after that (birth of the
> children). I did little things but never a real job. That's
> why I'm poor. My husband had mustard gas in the war. He
> was a sick man. I did what I could. I took care of myself.

> Now, I live with my son. I mind my own business. I do my cooking, washing. The walking, that's my biggest problem.

Mrs. A.T., who was 88-years old, related how she had left school at age 15 and worked picking vegetables, cleaning houses and in night clubs. Later, she had a saleswoman's job which she greatly enjoyed.

> There isn't anything different I would have wanted. I didn't have much money growing up. It's just the way it was. I loved my job selling. There isn't another job I would have liked better. When the husband didn't work out with the drinking, I left. I've always been happy.

Another woman described how she felt about her present life.

> I get down some days, thinking how no one comes by and how I can't do the ceramics anymore. But I guess I'm lucky. I'm in my own home and I can still dress myself.

Although she had lost the opportunity for creative expression and connecting with others, maintaining some degree of independence was important. The process of *Making Do* involved an element of acceptance of life as it was and as it is now. Most of the women had functional limitations but still worked at maintaining themselves in their homes, connecting with others and preserving a degree of independence. They drew upon past experiences as well as the present to make sense of their lives.

Although many of the women expressed feelings that could be viewed as satisfaction with life, those that indicated otherwise nevertheless wished to continue living as long as possible. George and Clipp (1991) suggested that some adults may find life unsatisfying but they still found it meaningful and, in that sense, could be aging well. The striving for connectedness with others and maintaining their independence appeared to give purpose to the lives of the participants.

Frankl (1985) observed that each situation encountered throughout life could be viewed as a chance to fulfill life's meaning. He described how to acquire this meaning in life through achieving tasks, responding to experiences such as watching a sunset, or accepting one's situation in life. The women in the present study seemed to accept functional limitations while continuing to attempt tasks that observing health professionals might consider impossible.

They continued to experience life by interacting with others or watching activity through a window. Their acceptance of their situation did not indicate a giving up but rather a daily meeting of challenges. What made this process a *Making Do* was that the lack of finances, social contacts, or functional abilities did not produce a sense of helplessness or a lack of purpose in their lives. Their chief goal appeared to be maintaining the self.

What emerged from the women's self description and how they accomplished their daily living generated the concept of *Able Self* which can be viewed as the actor that engages in *Making Do*. These women saw themselves as able although limited in some areas. As Mrs. T.E. noted:

> I do all my work in my place. I can walk a little but I need
> some help.

Her abilities were related to the environment in which she functioned. While able in her own place, she needed assistance in other environments.

Although, Mrs. A.T. gave up dancing, she was still active in the community and considered herself as an individual with few limitations:

> I model for the church. I can still do everything.

Another participant, Mrs. R.K. compared herself to other elderly persons who were younger than herself:

> I like to play cards on Thursday night, as long as I get a
> ride. It's a mixed group, men and women. I'm the oldest
> but they don't seem to mind. Other than my legs having
> trouble walking, I do the same as them.

When asked what activities were hardest to give up as she became older, Mrs. G.F. responded that she had not changed them. Later, however, she related being unable to perform housekeeping chores.

> I think I've always been active. Don't think there are other
> things I would want to do. I get around. Since I broke my
> hip a while ago, I use a cane. Can't do the vacuuming. I get
> a woman in to do that. I walk around the house but I can't
> reach the shelves too good.

This participant did not see herself as slowing down but as continuing to be active. The fact that she required some assistance with chores in the home did not seem to bother her.

Mrs. R.B. stated that the loss of some activities were gradual. Even though there were some activities she no longer performed, she perceived herself as doing better than most people her age.

> I'm doing all right. I still drive. I have a few problems but
> they aren't too bad. I can manage better than most.

As a cohort, the study participants experienced various common stresses in their lives such as, two world wars and the Great Depression of the 1930s. In addition, many of them faced illness, economic struggles, and losses of relationships. Nonetheless, they emerged as survivors and as able selves who mastered life's stresses.

Younger (1991) explored the theory of self mastery as follows:

> Mastery is a human response to difficult or stressful
> circumstances in which competency, control and
> dominance have been gained over the experience of stress.
> It means having developed new capabilities, having
> changed the environment and or reorganized the self so
> that there is a meaning and purpose in living that
> transcends the difficulty of the experience and emerges
> with greater strength and resilience. . . . It is a personal
> resource that enables one to imagine oneself as capable of
> acting effectively on the environment to meet one's felt
> needs. (p.81)

As shown, the women in the present study described themselves as able to carry out their activities of life. If necessary, they enlisted whatever assistance was required while seeking to maintain mastery over their lives.

Three categories were identified within the process of *Making Do*: 1) Limiting Losses, 2) Creating New Spaces and 3) A Slowing Down — But Not a Giving Up.

Limiting Losses. Limiting losses was a mechanism that allowed these women to engage successfully in the process of *Making Do*. Elder (1991) noted that the Great Depression represented a common and profound experience of loss for women in this age group.

> Family life in the thirties often entailed severe income reductions and prolonged unemployment, disability, death or separation of a spouse. Old age has much in common with such events. . . . Hence we believe that Depression hardship offered a potential form of apprenticeship for women in learning to cope with the inevitable losses of old age. (p.13)

Limiting losses can be related to maintaining independence in daily activities. Even when total independence was not possible, the women struggled to remain at the present level. Mrs. A.B. accepted a certain amount of dependence in order to preserve a degree of independence:

> Even if I need his help to shower, I try to do as much as I can. I get weak so I have him help me to the shower chair. Then he goes out and I wash. He helps me out and then I get dressed. It takes a long time some days. Have to go slow. But I feel good if I can just get myself dressed.

Another participant, Mrs. M.M., continued to do what she was capable of.

> On a good day, I go to the back stairs, a few steps down and hang the wash. The couple who helps me out would do it but if I can, I want to.

Decreased functional ability in activities of daily living has been documented as a predictor of future institutionalization. Katz et al. (1983) noted that most non institutionalized elderly people were independent in the basic functions of daily living. Therefore, the struggle to maintain whatever level of independence in function they had was an attempt to maintain mastery over their own bodies. A significant finding from Katz's study was that once independent functions were lost, they usually did not return in the older age groups. Therefore, maintaining even partial independence was crucial, since incremental losses could lead to total dependence.

The study participants also limited physical losses by averting potential dangers. At times, this involved avoiding an unsafe activity within their home or an external unsafe environment. As Mrs. G.D. explained:

> After dark, I don't go out. It's not safe. They see you don't walk too good. They can push you down and rob you.

The women were generally afraid of falling and thus took preventive measures. Many avoided going out in the snow and ice. One participant verbalized:

> I can't get out when the weather is bad because I could fall.

Another 92-year old women who used a cane, had a problem with dizziness and was in fear of falling. She stated that she did not go out alone.

> I wait for my daughter. On Sundays, she comes and we go to dinner. But the rest of the week, I stay inside. I could go backwards on the stairs and fall.

The limiting of losses was also seen in relation to holding on to possessions. Mrs. R.K. noted the following in regard to piles of papers around the house:

> All this stuff. C. (daughter) gets upset sometimes and wants to clean it up. If it's all put away, I can't find it. I keep it out. This reminds me of what I have to do.

Another participant, who lived with her husband, held on to her house and possessions. She was attempting to maintain herself as long as she could in her own home. Here's how she described her situation:

> My sons don't live here. One is in Florida, the other in Maine. But they say come live with us. Maybe we should

> but we don't want to give this house up. We had this house
> built. I would have to give up my furniture and all the
> things I've saved.

Possessions to the study population meant ownership and a degree of control over their environment. The participant cited above had many objects about her home that represented important times in her life. She was attempting to create a *holding pattern* with her possessions close by as part of her struggle to maintain some independence.

The participants also had developed certain routines in their lives. Reich and Zautra (1991) suggested that routinization, which involved the structuring of time and daily events, was a relatively independent trait unrelated to other personality traits. Routinization put daily life into a type of order that could increase the person's sense of control. Although the women did not seem adverse to surprise events, they performed their activities on a daily and weekly basis within a specific time frame.

It could be concluded that the routinization of the days and weeks may have been a way of limiting the loss of energy of the participants and reducing their energy consumption by planning for activities. As one participant described her daily and weekly activities:

> I get up about 6:00 a.m. Don't sleep too good so I get up
> early. Fix myself a little something to eat. Tea, maybe
> cereal. Then I make my bed and tidy up a little. Then I rest
> a little. Four days a week, I go to the center. Fridays, I
> have my hair done. On Saturday, I do my wash and a little
> vacuuming. By 10:00 p.m., I'm ready for bed but I wake up
> on and off.

Creating New Spaces. The second category developed within the process of Making Do was the creating of new spaces. These women found spiritual spaces that involved a private worship with a personal god. Eighty-nine-year old Mrs. M.R. stated:

> I feel happy. Not afraid. I don't do anything bad. I take
> good care of the kids. . . . If something on my mind not
> good, I go out in the yard. I work. Jesus is my boss. I pray
> every morning. My legs hurt too much to go to church.

Mrs. G.D. also spoke of praying within her home because she couldn't get to her church:

> I belong to the Episcopal Church but I can't get there. I would like to. I pray by myself.

Another participant, Mrs. O.P. said:

> I listen to mass on Sunday. I listen to two masses. I'm a shut-in. It's the best I can do. I say my prayers. God takes care of me.

Another women described how she reconciled her feelings about God and death.

> I try not to let things bother me. Sometimes I think what the heck am I doing here. Then I worry whether God is going to take me upstairs or if I'll spend some time downstairs. But I don't worry too much. No use. I can't change anything. I was a good mother to my children. I always worked hard. I was never mean to anyone. I don't go to church anymore unless the children take me. Otherwise, I pray at home.

Courtenay, Poon, Martin, Clayton and Johnson (1992) described the results of a study in which they examined the religiosity of persons from ages 60 to 100 and over. They found that as a person ages, religion increases in importance as a coping mechanism. Many of the centenarians in their study believed that the future was in God's hands. A similar observation was noted about the women in the present study although the mean age was 89 years. They seemed to have made peace with the type of worship they were engaged in as well as their relationship with God.

Blazer (1991) pointed out that answers to one's personal meaning in life were individual and that spirituality often provided the framework within which elderly people evaluated the meaning of the later years. No longer able to engage in organized religious activities, the study participants made their own personal spaces in which to conduct their own worship.

Also of significance were the new physical spaces these women created in their environments. For many it meant moving from their homes to live in subsidized housing or with adult children. Shared living quarters, however, did not generally prove to be a satisfactory arrangement. Most of the women in this type of situation would have preferred to live alone. Even when their apartment was an ordinary city- subsidized building, the participants described their places quite positively. One woman asked the researcher to go to her "place" with her. Opening the door, she said "Isn't it great!" The furniture was worn, the rug frayed, and the paint a dismal beige. There were ceramics and photographs, however, on every flat surface.

The woman had created a space that was hers. Surrounded by her belongings, she felt in touch with her place, a sense of ownership. The positive attitude of this participant contrasted sharply with the response of Mrs. M. who shared the home she owned with her daughter and son in law. Compared to other homes where the subjects lived alone, this residence was neat and uncluttered and devoid of pictures, papers or any personal objects.

Mrs. M.I. noted that she lived with her daughter and her husband, but "It's my house. I try to stay out of their way." When asked how she felt about her life, she replied:

> Well, like I told you. Getting out is what I miss most and I
> wish I was just able to live in my place by myself. But I
> need help.

According to Kart (1990) older people were likely to have a more positive attitude toward their homes as well as a greater attachment than younger people. When an individual lived alone, that space had a clear personal designation. This factor could reinforce the person's sense of her own identity. 92-year old participant described what was most important to her:

> A place of my own, that's what matters most. Taking care
> of myself as long as I can.

As they grew older, most of the women indicated that they had changed their place of residence. They voiced their reasons as either an inability to maintain a large home or the need to be near an adult child for assistance. Adapting to a new residence seemed to have been satisfactory when it contained their own possessions.

Wapner, Demuck and Redondo (1990) suggested that cherished possessions served adaptive functions as comforters and anchor points, providing a place for spiritual relationships and a sense of belongingness. Although their study involved nursing home patients, it could be concluded that in an environmental transition, cherished possessions helped to create a new space with a personal identity.

New spaces may represent an environmental adaptation to a physical disability. At times, a space within the home changes function to provide ease of motion. To illustrate, one of the study participants converted the living room into an all- purpose room with a hospital bed for herself as well as certain objects within close reach. Often, the environment must *shrink* with rooms performing multiple functions. People created comfort zones in their homes. One participant described her adaptation as follows:

> I haven't been upstairs in years. I just can't do it. I have what I need down here nearby. Also the bathroom is down here, so that way I'm set too.

Kart (1990) made a credible point, noting that an individual's competence needed to fit with the environment where the person lived. When the fit was good, the competence of an individual would be consistent with the demands of the environment, and adaptation was positive.

A Slowing Down But Not A Giving Up. The aging process produces many biological changes that affect the way an individual functions. Physical aging as a long term gradual process was reflected in the comments of Mrs. R.B.:

> It's not like one day you can do something and then you can't. Like the curtains. It got harder and harder to get on the step stool, to get them down. Now I have someone do them.

The study participants readily spoke of activities taking longer to perform. As one woman stated:

> I do my own shopping. If I walk fast, I take a pill under my
> tongue. The pain in the chest slows me.

Another woman noted:

> I get up. I'm slow but I get dressed. Every day I go to the
> center that I can.

Sometimes these women described a lack of energy, as pointed out by
a 94-year old participant:

> I wanted to be independent. I would work now if I could.
> Even now I still do a little alterations. I can't see as well
> and I don't have that push. It's hard to explain but
> sometimes I just don't have it.

She also described her morning when she took time to perform
activities:

> It takes me awhile to get going. I make my own breakfast.
> I tidy up a little. I need help with vacuuming. Otherwise, I
> can manage. If I get tired, I just lay down.

One 89-year old woman mentioned how long simple dressing took:

> It takes a long time some days. I have to go slow. I feel
> good if I can just get myself dressed.

Williams and Bird (1992) studied locomotion in healthy older
and younger adults. Their findings showed consistent age-related
differences in the speed that individuals used in walking and stair
climbing. They suggested that there might be a general and possibly
inevitable slowing of the maximum output of the motor system. This
process accompanied by other changes such as a decreased cardiac
output, contributed to the slowing down of activity performance.
Normal physical aging changes compounded by chronic arthritis and
heart disease tended to result in an older person being unable to
perform at the same speed as a younger person, whether cooking,
dressing or walking. Peterson (1994) noted that as people age they
become less alike. This factor along with individual variability in

coping skills may account for the processes observed in the study group.

Rest periods and the use of a slower pace enabled study participants to accomplish their daily activities of living. They did not relinquish performing activities readily and continued to perform what was necessary for self maintenance. Giving up tasks too stressful or dangerous, such as yard work, climbing ladders or heavy housework, was a healthy coping strategy to preserve energy for other activities as well as prevent injuries. These women were able people who slowed down in response to physical aging but did not give up.

Summary

This research yielded a substantive theory which described how twenty women participants created meaning in their lives through activity. The type of theory was differentiated from formal theory in being less prone to generalization; also, it was derived from a particular substantive area under study. Substantive theories aim to generate new grounded formal theories and to reformulate previously established ones (Glaser and Strauss 1967).

The building of the theory began with identifying two concepts early in the data gathering phase. As was appropriate for a grounded theory study, the data were analyzed as obtained by the investigator. What evolved were consistent themes related to connectedness and independence.

As cited by the study population, the activities most difficult to relinquish as well as those of the greatest importance were the ones that enabled the participants to reflect these themes. A definition of activity from the perspective of these women was also sought. It was described in a personal way, relating to physical and mental processes as well as experiences.

From the data provided by participants, it was possible to identify an *Able Self*. This concept evolved from the core category of *Making Do* which, in turn, represented the foundation of the substantive theory.

The *Making Do* category became visible through a line by line analysis that involved asking questions of the data: What activity is being carried out here? Under what conditions is it occurring? What seems to be going on?

Employing the core variable of *Making Do* made it possible to determine how the women in the study created meaning in their lives through activity. They did not give up but rather met daily challenges as they continued to experience life. Their responses to the *Making Do* category were further illustrated in the three subcategories of Limiting Losses, Creating New Spaces, and a Slowing Down But Not a Giving Up. By being successful at achieving the Making Do, the *Able Self* becomes reinforced.

V

CONCLUSIONS, IMPLICATIONS AND RECOMMENDATIONS

Summary of Findings

One of the most remarkable trends in the last few decades has been the steady growth of the elderly in the American population. Their longevity no longer remains at a plateau, since an increasing number, mostly women, are beginning to reach the age of 85 and over. As people get older, new challenges face them created by the inevitability of personal losses, changing lifestyles, and chronic illness.

In recent times, the literature has revealed a marked interest in the elderly studied from a variety of perspectives. Although several studies have dealt with the functional activities of these people, little attempt has been made to explore their meaning to the individual and particularly the older woman. The present study was designed to gain some understanding of how women in the over 85 age group are able to make sense of their lives through activities. Employing the existentialist framework of Viktor Frankl, it was based on the assumption that life holds a potential for meaning for each individual. Activities were interpreted as opportunities to create meaning.

Twenty women, ranging in age from 85 to 105 years, shared their life experiences for the research. The first of three research questions addressed the following: How did women age 85 and over define activity? In this light, each participant was approached to define activity in her own words. Overall, the women related it to their present existence, defining activity as a personal life process. None of the group described themselves as inactive or not engaging in any activities.

The second research question sought to elicit the nature of the activities. It was determined that those activities the women chose to participate in on a regular basis fostered a sense of connectedness and independence. Connecting with others, whether within the family or through social interaction outside the home, appeared to be important to the participants.

Under connecting, the first subcategory that evolved dealt with outside social activities and was named *superficial connecting*, which described two types, parallel and cooperative. A parallel activity such as Bingo enabled the study population, even those with limited mobility, to connect with others. Cooperative activities were undertaken by the women who attended a senior center or group regularly, and who had specific roles such as participating in the planning of an activity.

A second subcategory, named *hesitant outsider*, related to the type of connecting that occurred within the family unit. Even when the women lived with their families, they were reluctant to seek out and connect with relatives to the extent that they desired. Many had a need for more and better family interaction but hesitated to verbalize this.

The second category included activities that produced a sense of independence. It generated three subcategories described as relinquished activities, marginal activities, and adequate activities.

Work performed in the past outside the home was cited as an important example of relinquished activities. Many missed working, which they would have liked to continue if it were possible. Another relinquished activity, but one that seemed to have little impact for the women, was heavy housework. Family or paid assistance appeared to remedy the situation.

A second subcategory involved marginal activities performed by the women, such as food preparation and walking outdoors, which often required partial assistance. These were activities that most of the participants could do without assistance and included bathing, dressing, and light housekeeping. This particular category was thus labeled as *adequate*. Meriting a similar description was the activity identified as the mental processes.

Many women noted that the ability to function well mentally was the most important activity for them to retain. The entire study population was able to make appropriate decisions on a daily basis and maintain a safe environment.

The third research question represented the core of the study in seeking to ascertain how the activities of the participants helped to create meaning in their lives. Identified as *Making Do,* this activity involved an acceptance of life as it used to be and as it currently existed. It reflected a meeting of life's challenges on a daily basis.

The adjustment to a *Making Do* showed that the lack of financial resources, social contacts, or functional abilities did not produce a sense of helplessness or lack of purpose. Although many of the women recognized their limitations, they perceived themselves as *able*" This *Able Self* became the impetus for fostering the activity of Making Do. From this category flowed three subcategories identified as limiting losses, creating new spaces, and a slowing down but not a giving up.

Conclusions

It can be concluded that the women in the study sought to maintain activities of connectedness and independence. They wanted to be among people and made an effort to continue to engage in activity involving others. Although few had deep relationships outside the family, the superficial friendships they had seemed to motivate them to venture beyond their home.

Most of the women lived alone and preferred that arrangement. Although they desired more interaction with family members, it was difficult for them to seek it. Thus, the amount and quality of interaction within the family did not fulfill their expectations. Family members, however, such as children, nieces and nephews seemed to provide for the necessary activities that participants were unable to perform. They tended to the food shopping, heavy housework, and transportation for medical care but often overlooked the psychosocial needs of the women.

How the person fitted within the environment appeared important to the self maintenance of the women in their homes. They created spaces that permitted safe functioning. Most of them spoke of the need to rest, move slowly, and space the timing of activities. It was essential for them to have objects within close reach, barrier-free passageways, and level surfaces which reduced energy expenditure and ensured greater security.

The activities of daily living, such as bathing and dressing, were particularly important to the women. This was not only because they were necessary when living alone (as most did), but to help reinforce feelings of self worth. The participants focused much of their time and energy on self maintenance. This mastery of the self did not imply a withdrawal from others since they participated in activities to be among people. The women were able to *Make Do* with limited functional ability and viewed themselves as *able* within their own environments.

The results of this research support Frankl's work on meaning in life. Women in the present investigation drew upon past activities to create meaning as they aged. They spoke of how they raised children, performed good work, and often put their own goals aside to care for their families. Their revelations were consistent with Frankl's (1985) in noting that "nothing and nobody can deprive and rob us of what we have safely delivered and deposited in the past." (p.42)

The study population faced chronic illness, economic decline and loss of function by *Making Do*. Frankl (1986) also pointed out that a way of giving life meaning was through attitudinal values. The participants continued to experience the world about them, enjoying being among people, watching them, and just sitting in their own places. Such experiences, according to Frankl (1986), helped them to realize values. He further observed that people give meaning to their lives by achieving tasks. The study participants sought to remain as independent as possible to accomplish their daily activities of living.

Implications

The resources of a given community can play an important role in maintaining the health and well being of its residents. This observation is particularly relevant to the needs of a growing older population.

In the present study, the participants who lived alone could maintain themselves partly because of low cost subsidized housing and meals that were provided in a senior center or delivered to their homes. Although transportation was available in varying degrees, overall improvement was indicated. The women had difficulty walking long distances as well as waiting for buses, which proved to be a major deterrent to participating in outside activities.

Professionals practicing in the public health arena have a responsibility to evaluate the resources available to an elderly population. The delivery of a comprehensive patient care system requires a familiarity with the organizational structures that offer the appropriate services to assist clients and their families. Equally critical is an astuteness about the political nature of the community and the sources exerting the proper clout to assist with programs, projects and funding activities to enhance the quality of life of older people.

Nurse-managed centers providing primary care represent a growing trend. Strategically placed in a community, they are accessible and offer efficient low cost services. Many serve a large geriatric population and appear to be a logical resource for clients like the women in the study. Most are staffed by nurse practitioners and others with advanced practice skills.

In exploring issues regarding the elderly, professionals need to consider barrier-free low cost housing, prepared meals, and accessible transportation. With their skill and expertise, they can make a valuable contribution as consultants or volunteers in the work of local advocate groups or chapters (such as the American Association of Retired Persons) devoted to the concerns of the older population.

In this study, the participants desired an increase in the quality and amount of interaction within the family. Health professionals such as nurses, physicians, and social workers should be able to assess the communication that takes place in the home, or at the senior center, and intervene as appropriate with the parties involved. Understanding family dynamics should facilitate the process. Also, professionals can suggest ways to improve communication, such as encouraging clients to verbalize their needs to the family. During the study, one participant sadly related what may be true for many older women: "No one has listened to me this long in years." Butler et al (1995) have noted that significant gaps remain in the education of physicians in regards to women's health. The same situation has also existed in the education of professional nurses and social workers.

Safety is another important consideration for elderly people who live at home. By employing more than functional ability assessment tools, professionals will be able to determine how safe and secure are the living conditions and how adept clients are at caring for themselves.

Observing how clients meet their self care needs in the home setting will reveal how essential requirements are being met and if needed assistance is available through outside agencies, adult children, or paid help. The present study showed that even some of the oldest participants were quite resourceful in accomplishing what otherwise appeared to be impossible tasks.

One participant was legally blind and needed a walker for ambulation. Yet, she was mentally competent and able to take her medication correctly, and obtained meals and housekeeping services with outside assistance. Although this woman would have scored low on a functional ability instrument, she managed to be safe in her home.

An interesting study finding was the way in which the women limited their losses. To them, such activities as bathing and dressing were important, and even performing partial self care, created a feeling of mastery. How the older woman responds to activity losses would seem to have implications for nurses in planning the personal care of individuals in long term care settings.

An insightful observation derived from the research was the value of work to the participants. Work seemed to provide them with feelings of independence, and an opportunity for social interaction and economic rewards. The relinquished activity of paid work outside the home represented a major loss. This has particular implications for social workers who can assess prior work performed by older people and encourage them, if practical to develop new skills. Although paid work may not be a possibility for some age 85 and over, they may none the less be helped to engage in useful volunteer work that will increase their sense of self worth and dignity.

The "keeping of the mind" was important to the participants who valued their mental prowess. Professionals therefore, should be aware of what mental alertness means to these people, realizing that subtle changes in behavior might be attributed primarily to a correctable physical problem. One way of maintaining a person's mental status, even for the homebound client, is to arrange for outside contact. Older persons can be placed in touch with a friendly caller or visitor program. Conversations with others may provide an opportunity for continued stimulation and preserving function. The experienced clinician can be very valuable in assisting older persons to maintain function. Monitoring for subtle changes in cognition and intervening appropriately is the responsibility of all professionals who care this age group.

In order to find meaning in their activities as they age, older women may be in special need of assistance. They are often adjusting to widowhood and need help to find new roles that do not require a partner. Peterson (1994) notes that ultimately it means helping older persons find a reason for getting up each day.

Implications for Education

In the realm of health education, it can be predicted that students will be exposed to more geriatric clients during their preparation. Educators will have to broaden the academic base to accommodate new directions in the care of the elderly. No longer can this population be viewed as homogenous since people age differently — an important fact that professionals need to recognize. Also, the shift from acute to chronic disorders will require new and innovative modalities in delivering patient care.

Fresh challenges will be evident in the curriculum as faculty become au courant with the changing social scene that includes in particular a higher proportion of the well elderly. It, therefore, will be desirable to develop appropriate learning experiences for students early in their programs, in which they observe first hand the life-styles and adjustments of older individuals in the community.

Recommendations for Further Research

The present study involved women whose earlier life experiences occurred during significant events in the nation's history. They shared a commonality of living through two world wars and a Great Depression that created hard times. It can only be speculated that these situations had an impact upon them since all people are products of their times and experiences. What is known, however, from the data on the participants and reflected in their own words, was not only their perceptions of activity at the present time but their feelings about past experiences.

It can be surmised that an elderly population forty years hence may produce a study group with a perspective quite different from those of the women in the present study. Middle-aged people in the 1990s are exposed to influences quite different from those experienced by the women some decades ago. Progress in science, technology, a global society and other phenomenal advances have altered value systems and life-styles. For future work on the elderly, longitudinal studies beginning with a younger sample should be considered to produce useful data on the responses of people to life events as they age.

Many individuals currently live to age 85 and beyond. When they reach these advanced ages, their adult children are often in their fifties and sixties and beginning to plan retirement. Qualitative research is suggested that focuses on both the needs of the adult children and the elderly parent. Although adult children of elderly persons may help out as much as possible, it is evident that communication patterns can be improved.

Further research is also needed to provide alternate plans for home care. This is sorely needed in situations where the caregiver may also be over age 65 and dealing with chronic disease and disability. Topinkova (1994) suggests that what is needed is an integration of home and institutional care with innovations such as day care and temporary admissions. Research that focuses on comparing the cost effectiveness of these alternative means of elderly care is needed to provide documentation for reimbursement. There was a general lack of expression of anger among the participants. This may have been related to an inability or reluctance to express anger or resentment. Another reason may have been that the lack of expression of negative feelings was part of the act of Making Do. These women may have had limited expectations and therefore were more accepting of adverse life situations. Although the participants were asked about the difficulty of giving up activities, more direct questioning in future research pertaining to giving up activities may yield important information related to feelings of anger.

Other research may involve conducting studies in long term care facilities to determine the effect of planned programs of partial independence on the well being of clients. Also, the use of triangulation methods that combine both quantitative and qualitative methodology may provide useful perspectives about how older women carry out their activities of life and make sense of their worlds.

Another area for exploration is research including men of the same age group. The way in which older men describe how activities create meaning in their lives has the potential for adding to the body of knowledge related to gender similarities and differences.

Finally, the present study was undertaken because of the dearth of research on women age 85 and older. For further theory development, studies need to be conducted with a variety of populations of women age 85 and older. The study participants shared many similarities in terms of ethnic backgrounds, geographic locations and income levels. It is recommended that future research include populations of older women, such as minority women, urban and rural residents and representatives of a variety of income levels.

References

Acker, J. 1978. Issues in the sociological study of women's work. In *Women working*. A. Stromberg and S. Harkess. 134-161. Palo, California: Mayfield.

Almind, G. 1985. Risk factors in eighty-plus year olds living at home: An investigation of a Danish community. *International Journal of Aging and Human Development*. No. 3: 227-236.

American Association of Retired Persons. 1991. Facts about older women: Twelve powerful statistics on older woman. *AARP, Women's Initiative* 1.

American Association of Retired Persons. 1991. Facts about older women, income and poverty. *AARP, Women's Initiative* 1-2.

Aniansson, A., A. Rundgren and L. Sperling. 1980. Evaluation of functional capacity in activities of daily living in 70 year old men and women. *Scandinavian Journal of Rehabilitative Medicine* 12: 145-154.

Beauvoir de, S. 1989. *The second sex*. New York: Vintage Books.

Becker, P.H. 1993. Common pitfalls in published grounded theory research. *Qualitative Health Research*. 3, No. 2: 254-260.

Belenky, M.F., B.C. Clinchy, N.R. Goldberger and J.M. Tarule. 1986. *Women's ways of knowing*. New York: Basic Books.

Blau, F.D. 1978. The data on women workers, past, present and future. In *Women working*. A. Stromberg and S. Harkess (Eds). 29-63. Palo Alto: Mayfield.

Blazer, D. 1991. Spiritually and aging well. *Generations* (winter): 61-68.

Blumer, H. 1969. *Symbolic interactionism — Perspective and method*. Englewood Cliffs: Prentice Hall.

Bogden, R.C. and S.K. Bilken 1982. *Qualitative research for education, An introduction to theory and methods*. Boston: Allyn and Baron Inc.

Burns, N. and S. Grove. 1993 *Nursing research: Conduct, critique and utilization*. New York: W.B. Sanders.

Branch, L.G. and A.R. Meyers 1987. Assessing physical function in the elderly. *Clinics in Geriatric Medicine*. 3, No. 1: 29-31.

Breckinridge, S.P. 1972. *Women in the twentieth century — A study of their political, social and economic activities*. New York: Arno Press.

Bruner, J. 1979. *On knowing.* Cambridge, Mass.: Belknap Press of Harvard University Press.

Burdman, M.G. 1986. *Healthful aging.* Englewood Cliffs: Prentice Hall.

Butler, R.N., S. Collins, D.E. Meier, C.F. Muller and V.W. Pinn. (1993) Older women's health: Taking the pulse's reveals gender gap in medical care. *Geriatrics.* 50, No. 5: 39-47

Carp, F.M. and D.L. Christensen. (1986) Older women living alone. *Research on Aging.* 8, No. 3: 407-425.

Cauley, J.A., R.E. La Port, R.B. Sandler, M.M. Schiamm and A.M. Kristea. 1987. Comparison of methods to measure physical activity in postmenopausal women. *American Journal of Clinical Nutrition.* 45: 14-22.

Cohen, E.S. 1988. The elderly mystique— Constraints on the autonomy of the elderly with disabilities. *The Gerontologist.* 28, No. 6: 24-31.

Copeland, J.R.M., M.J. Kelleher, A.M.R. Smith and P. Devlin. 1986. The well, the mentally ill, the old and the old old, A community survey of elderly persons in London. *Aging and Society.* 6: 417-433.

Courtenay, B.C., L.W. Poon, P. Martin, G.M. Clayton and M.A. Johnson. 1982. Religiosity and adaptation in the oldest old. *International Journal Aging and Human Development.* 34, No. 1: 47-56.

Chenitz, W.C. and J. Swanson. 1986. *From practice to grounded theory.* Menlo Park, CA.: Addison Wesley.

Cumming, E. and W. Henry. 1961. *Growing old: The process of disengagement.* New York: Basic Books.

Creelman, M.B. 1966. *The experimental investigation of meaning.* New York: Springer.

Darkenwald, G.G. 1980. Field research and grounded theory. In *Changing approaches to studying adult education,* H.B. Long, 63-77. San Francisco: Jossey-Bass.

Devault, M. 1990. Talking and listening from a women's standpoint — Feminist strategies for interviewing and analysis. *Social Problems.* 37, No. 1: 96-113.

Elder Jr., G.H. 1991. Making the best of life: Perspectives on lives, times and aging. *Generations.* (winter): 12-17.

Ehrhardt, A. 1985. The psychology of gender. In *Gender and the life course,* A. Rossi (Ed.). 81-96. Hawthorne, N.Y.: Aldine.

Epstein, C.F. 1989. Workplace boundaries, conceptions and creations. *Social Research.* 56, No. 3: 572-590.

Euler, B. 1992. A flaw in gerontological assessment: The weak relationship of elderly superficial life satisfaction to deep psychological well-being. *International Journal of Aging and Human Development.* 34, No. 4: 299-310.

Fielding, N.G. and J.L. Fielding. 1986. *Linking data, qualitative research methods.* (4) Beverly Hills: Sage.

Folbre, N. and M. Abel. 1989. Women's work and women's households: Gender bias in the U.S. census. *Social Research.* 56, No. 3: 546-569.

Ford, A.B., L.J. Folmar, R.B. Solomon, J.H. Medalie, A.W. Roy, and S.S. Galazka. 1988. Health and function in the old and very old. *Journal of the American Geriatric Society.* 36, No. 3: 187-197.

Frankl, V.E. 1985. *The unconscious god.* New York: Washington Square Press.

Frankl, V.E. 1985. *The unheard cry for meaning.* New York: Washington Square Press.

Frankl, V.E. 1986. *The doctor and the soul.* New York: Random House.

Gallo, J.J., W. Reichel and L. Anderson. 1995 *Handbook of geriatric assessment.* Gaithersburg, Maryland: Aspen

George, L.K. and E.C. Clipp. Subjective components of aging well. *Generations.* (winter): 57-60.

Gilligan, C. 1982. *In a different voice.* Cambridge: Harvard University Press.

Glaser, B.G. and A.L. Strauss. 1967. *The discovery of grounded theory.* Chicago: Aldine.

Golant, S.M. 1984. *A place to grow old, The meaning of environment in old age.* New York: Columbia University Press.

Gregory, M.D. 1983. Occupational behavior and life satisfaction among retirees. *The American Journal of Occupational Therapy.* 37, No. 8: 548-551.

Hall, A.M. 1985. Knowledge and gender: Epistemological questions in the social analysis of sport. *Sociology of Sport Journal.* 2, No. 3: 25-41.

Hammersley, M. and P. Atkinson. 1983. *Ethnography principles in practice.* London: Tavistock.

Havighurst, R., B.L. Neugarten and S.S. Tobin. 1968. Disengagement and patterns of aging. In *Middle age and aging,* B. Neugarten (Ed), Chicago: The University of Chicago Press.

Harding, S. and M.B. Hintikka. 1983. *Discovering reality — feminist perspectives on epistemology metaphysics, methodology, and philosophy of science.* Holland: D. Reidel.

Harding, S. 1986. *The science question in feminism.* Ithaca, N.Y.: Cornell University Press.

Haug, M.R. and J.J. Folmar. 1986. Longevity gender and life quality. *Journal of Health and Social Behavior.* 27, No. 4: 332-345.

Heinemann, A.W., A. Colorez, S. Frank and D. Taylor. 1988. Leisure activity participation of elderly individuals with low vision. *The Gerontologist.* 28, No. 2: 181-184.

Herzog, A.R., K.C. Holden and N.M. Seltzer. (Eds.). 1989. *Health and economic status of older women.* New York: Baywood.

Herzog, A.R. 1989. Physical and mental health in older women: Selected research issues and data sources. In *Health and economic status of older women,* A.R. Herzog, K.C. Holden and N.M. Seltzer. (Eds.). 35-91. New York: Baywood.

Hoeffer, B. 1987. Predictors of life outlook of older single women. *Research in Nursing and Health.* 10, No. 2: 111-117.

Holden, K. 1988. Poverty and living arrangements among older women. Are changes in economic well being underestimated? *Journal of Gerontological Society.* 43: 22-27.

Hulicka, I.M., J.B. Morganti, and J.F. Cataldo. 1975. Perceived latitude of choice of institutionalized elderly women. *Experimental Aging Research.* 1, No. 1: 27-39.

Hutchinson, S. 1993. Grounded theory: The method. *Nursing research: A qualitative perspective.* (2nd. edition), P. Munhall and C. Oiler Boyd. 180-212. New York: National League for Nursing Press.

Ingersoll-Dayton, B. and C. Talbott. 1992. Assessments of social support exchanges: Cognitions of the old-old. *International Journal of Aging and Human Development.* 35, No. 2: 125-143.

Johnson, L. 1987. *Biology.* Dubuque, Iowa: Wm. C. Brown.

Katz, S., L.G. Branch, J.A. Branson, J.A. Pasidero, J.C. Beck and D. S. Greer. 1983. Active life expectancy. *New England Journal of Medicine.* 309, No. 20: 1218-1224.

Katz, S. and M.W. Stroud. 1989. Functional assessment in geriatrics — A review of progress and directions. *Journal of the American Geriatrics Society.* 37, No. 3: 267-271.

Kart, C.S. 1990. *The realities of aging: An introduction to gerontology.* Massachusetts: Allyn and Bacon.

Kaufman, S.R. 1986. *The ageless self.* New York: First Meridian.

Kirk, J. and M.L. Miller. 1986. *Reliability and validity in qualitative research.* Beverly Hills: Sage Publications.

Krout, J. 1988. Rural versus urban differences in elderly parents contact with their children. *Gerontologist.* 28, No. 2: 198-203.

Lawton, M.P. and M. Fulcomer. 1987. Objective and subjective uses of time by older people. *International Journal of Aging and Human Development.* 24, No. 3: 171-188.

Lawton, M.P. 1983. Environment and other determinants of well being in older people. *The Gerontologist.* 23, No. 4: 349-357.

Lawton, M.P. 1991. Functional status and aging well. *Generations.* (winter): 31-34.

Leininger, M.M. (Ed.). 1985. *Qualitative research methods in nursing.* Orlando: Harcourt Brace Jovanich.

Lombranz, J., S. Bergman, N. Eyal and D. Shmotkin. 1988. Indoor and outdoor activities of aged women and men as related to depression and well being. *International Journal of Aging and Human Development.* 26, No. 4: 303-314.

Longino, C.F. 1988. Who are the oldest americans? *The Gerontologist.* 28, No. 4: 515-523.

Macdonald, B. and C. Rich. 1983. *Look me in the eye — Old women, aging and ageism.* San Francisco: Spinsters.

Maddox, G.L. 1991. Aging with a difference. *Generations.* (winter): 7-10.

Maddox, G.L. 1968. Persistence of life style among the elderly: A longitudinal study of patterns of social activity in relation to life satisfaction. In *Middle age and aging — A reader in social psychology,* B.L. Neugarten (Ed.). 181-183. Chicago: The University of Chicago Press.

Manton, K.G. 1988. A longitudinal study of functional change and mortality in the United States. *Journal of Gerontology.* 43, No. 5: 153-161.

Maxwell, J.A. 1992. Understanding and validity in qualitative research. *Harvard Educational Review.* 62, No. 3: 279-300.

McGuire, F. 1983. Constraints on leisure involvement in the later years. In *Activities and the well elderly,* P.M. Foster (Ed.). New York: Haworth Press.

Miles, M. and Huberman, A.M. 1984. *Qualitative data analysis.* Beverly Hills: Sage Publications.

Miller, J.B. 1986. *Toward a new psychology of women.* Boston: Beacon Press.

Neugarten, B.L. and S.S. Tobin. 1968. Personality and patterns of aging. In *Middle age and aging — A reader in social psychology,* B. Neugarten. 173-177. Chicago: The University of Chicago Press.

Oakley, A. 1974. *Women's work — the housewife, past and present.* New York: Vintage Books.

Ogden, C.K. and I.A. Richards. 1953. *The meaning of meaning.* New York: Harcourt, Brace and Co., Inc.

Oudt, B.M. 1988. Self reported health status and health behaviors of women aged 85 and older. (Doctoral dissertation, Rush University). *University Microfilm International.* No. 8818352.

Partridge, E. 1977. *A short etymological dictionary of modern english origins.* New York: Macmillan Publishing Co., Inc.

Pear, R. 1993. (June 13). Clinton's health-care plan: It's still big, but it's farther away. *The New York Times.* p. 4.

Peppers, L.G. 1976. Patterns of leisure and adjustment to retirement. *The Gerontologist.* 16, No. 5: 441-446.

Peterson, M. Physical aspects of aging: Is there such a thing as 'normal'?. Geriatrics. 49, No.2: 45-48.

Polanyl, M. 1962. *Personal knowledge — Towards a post critical philosophy.* Chicago: The University of Chicago Press.

U.S. Bureau of Census. 1992. *Statistical abstracts of the U.S., the national data book.* Washington, D.C.: U.S. Government Printing Office.

United Nations. 1991. *The world's women trends and statistics 1070-1990.* New York: United Nations.

Reich, J.W. and A.J. Zautra. 1991. Analyzing the trait of routinization in older adults. *International Journal Aging and Human Development.* 32, No. 3: 161-180.

Roberto, K. and P. Kimboko. 1989. Friendships in later life: Definitions and maintenance patterns. *International Journal of Aging and Human Development.* 28, No. 1: 9-18.

Rodeheaver, D. 1990. Labor market progeria. *Generations.* (summer): 53-58.

Roberts, H. 1988. *Doing feminist research.* London: Routledge.

Rodgers, W.L. and A.R. Herzog. 1987. Interviewing older adults: The accuracy of factual information. *Journal of Gerontology.* 42, No. 4: 387-394.

Rodin, J. 1986. Aging and health — Effects of control. *Science.* 233: 1271-1275.

Rosenthal, G and C.S. Landefeld. 1993. Do older medicare patients cost hospitals more? *Archives of Internal Medicine* 153, Jan 11

Rosenwaike, I. and A. Dolinsky. 1987 The changing demographic determinants of the growth of the extreme aged. *The Gerontologist.* 27: 275-280.

Rossi, A. 1985. Gender and parenthood. In *Gender and the life course,* A. Rossi. 161-192. Hawthorne, N.Y.: Aldine.

Rubenstein, L., D. Calkins, S. Greenfield, A. Jette, R. Meenan, M. Nevins, L. Rubenstein, J. Wasson, and M.E. William. 1989. Health status assessment for elderly patients. *Journal of the American Geriatrics Society.* 37, No. 6: 562-569.

Simonsick, E.M., M.E. Lafferty, C.L. Phillips, C.F. Mendes de Leon, S.V. Kasl, T.E. Seeman, G. Fillenbaum, P. Hebert, and J.H. Lemke. 1993. Risk due to inactivity in physically capable older adults. *The American Journal of Public Health.* 83, No. 10: 1443-1448.

Solomon R. and M. Peterson. 1994. Successful aging: How to help patients cope with change. *Geriatrics.* 49, No. 4: 41-47.

Stern, P.N. 1980. Grounded theory methodology its uses and processes. *Image.* 12, No. 1: 20-24.

Strauss, A. and J. Corbin. 1991. *Basics of qualitative research, grounded theory procedures and techniques.* Newbury Park, California: Sage.

Surrey, J. 1984. *Self in relation.* (working paper) Massachusetts: Stone Center, Wellesly College.

Taeuber, C. (Ed.). 1991. *Statistical handbook on women in America.* Arizona: Orynx Press.

The University of the State of New York, The State Education Department. 1993. *Equal opportunity for women.* Albany, New York: The State Education Department.

Thomas, J.L. 1992. *Adulthood and aging.* Boston: Allyn and Bacon, A Division of Simon and Schuster.

Tinsley, H., J.D. Teoff, S.L. Colbs and N. Kaufman. 1985. A system of classifying leisure activities in terms of the psychological benefits of participation reported by older persons. *Journal of Gerontology.* 40(2): 172-178.

Topinkova, E. 1994. Care for elders with chronic disease and disability. *Hastings Center Report.* September-October.

Vanek, J. 1978. Housewives as workers. In *Women working,* A. Stromberg and S. Harkess (Eds.). 392-416. Palo, California: Mayfield.

Wapner, S., J. Demick, and J.P. Redondo. 1990. Cherished possessions and adaption of older people to nursing homes. *International Journal Aging and Human Development.* 31, No. 3: 219-235.

Williams, K. and M. Bird. 1992. The aging mover: A preliminary report on constraints to action. *The International Journal Aging and Human Development.* 34, No. 3: 241-255.

Williams, M.E., N.M. Hadler and J.A. Earp. 1982. Manual ability as marker of dependency in geriatric women. *Journal of Chronic Disease.* 35, No. 2: 115-122.

Younger, J.B. 1991. A theory of mastery. *Advances in Nursing Science.* 1: 76-79.

Appendix A

VIGNETTES

The purpose of the following section is provide the reader with information about the background of the study participants as well as fresh insights into their thoughts and concerns. These vignettes show the commonalties in life-style, attitudes and adjustments that occur in people as they reach their later years. They represent the impressions of the researcher made during the interview process.

Participant #1

Mrs. A.B. age 89, lives with her husband of the same age in their own ranch home located in a residential neighborhood. The one-level house has six steps at the front entrance and at the rear through the garage. Their furniture looks old with the covers slightly frayed and the carpeting showing some wear. The rooms are well lit, neat and uncluttered. Photographs of people of different ages are visible.

Born in New York City as one of eleven children, Mrs. A.B. was raised primarily by her mother since her father died when she was eight years old. After completing two years of high school, she began working. At age 22, she married and two years later had her first child. When she was 48 years old, her husband insisted that she leave her job as a manager in a department store. She had enjoyed the work and regretted not being able to continue.

Mrs. A.B. appears frail, weighing about 90 lbs. Unsteady in her gait, she uses a walker because of limited mobility. She previously enjoyed ceramic work at the senior center but can no longer get there due to her immobility and a problem with incontinence. Except for appointment with her physician, she rarely leaves home.

Both Mrs. A.B. and her husband receive meals-on-wheels and a cleaning woman biweekly. While Mr. A.B. gets social security and a pension, Mrs. A.B. has only social security. They have two sons who live out of state but maintain regular contact through letters and telephone calls.

Participant #2

Mrs. L.C., age 94 and a widow for twenty years, lives in a suburb of New York City in her own apartment located in the home of her daughter and son in law. Her rent is free but she pays her own telephone bill. She is assisted by social security which she earned for sporadic work, but her daughter provides some money to supplement her income.

Born in Brooklyn the second oldest of ten children, Mrs. L.C. completed the eighth grade and married at age 21. When she was seven she began "working," sewing on her mother's machine. Until recently she did alterations at home for payment, but at her son's insistence she continues with her sewing only as a favor to family members.

Mrs. L.C. dresses in bright colors and walks quickly without any assistive devices. The availability of a bus makes it possible for her to attend the center four days a week. At home, she can perform light housekeeping chores such as doing dishes and dusting while her daughter and granddaughter assist with any heavy housekeeping. Her son also maintains close touch with her.

Participant #3

Mrs. G.D., age 86, lives alone in a senior citizen's complex, which houses a senior center on the grounds. Inside the apartment building — a clean but sparse structure. Residents sitting on folding chairs and in wheelchairs occupy the lobby. Mrs. G.D.'s apartment appears gloomy with the blinds drawn and only a small lamp lit. It consists of an average-sized living room, one bedroom and a small kitchen.

Although the furniture looks worn, the apartment appears clean. Several pictures of family members adorn the living room. In the kitchen, small stacks of mail lay on the table. Throughout the area, a stale odor of cigarette smoke can be detected.

A native of New York City, Mrs. G.D. was one of four children raised by a single mother. Leaving school after the ninth grade, she went to work to help support her sisters and brothers. The jobs were mainly in factories. At age 18, she married and within a couple of years had two children whom she raised herself after leaving her alcoholic husband.

Continuing to work throughout her adult life, Mrs. G.D. earns social security as her primary source of income at the present time. However, she is able to work at the senior center for four hours twice a week which gives her added funds to alleviate some concern about paying bills.

Participant #4

Mrs. T.E., age 91, emigrated from Italy when she was ten years old. For the next four years, she attended a Catholic school and then went to work in a candy factory. Marrying at twenty, she subsequently had two children, and for the past 35 years has been a widow.

Slightly bent and walking with a cane, Mrs. T.E., dresses neatly with matching earrings and a necklace that complements her outfit. Because of poor vision, she can no longer sew, which was her main occupation - working at home - after her marriage and throughout her life. She attends the center two days a week, using the transportation provided.

Although Mrs. T.E. would prefer to live on her own if she could manage it, she appears satisfied with the present arrangement of having an apartment in her son's house. Through her husband's employment, she receives social security but no pension. Her daughter, who is in her late sixties, takes her shopping even though Mrs. T.E. believes she may be a burden. However, she pays for her own groceries as well as the telephone. Money, nonetheless, remains a concern.

Participant #5

Mrs. G.F. age 88, a native New Yorker, lives in subsidized housing in a suburban apartment and survives on her social security. She comes from a background of ten siblings and an alcoholic mother who died at forty-five years of age. An eighth grade graduate, she worked at various jobs until marrying at 18 and having two children, a daughter and son. She continued to work in different jobs, one time as a bottle washer in a hospital and another as a silk mill worker.

A small and neatly dressed woman, Mrs. G.F. attends the senior center as a major part of her daily life. There, at low cost, she has her lunch and brings her dinner home.

Since she was interviewed at the center no description of her home was obtained.

Her main support systems include her children, with her daughter assisting with the shopping. The senior center provides daily transportation.

Participant #6

Miss A.H., age 85 and a single woman, lives with her niece in a small ranch house located in a New York City residential suburb. During the interview, she was wearing a floral print cotton dress. The home was clean but appeared cluttered with children's toys. Only four steps are required to enter through the front door. Miss A.H. walked slowly but without any assistive devices.

Born in Italy, she was seven years old when she came to the United States with her parents and sister. After her mother died when Miss A.H. was ten, her father raised the two girls. She assumed the responsibility for her two young nieces when her sister died in her twenties, and considered herself a mother to them.

After completing two years of high school , she worked at various jobs. Between ages of 50 and 70, she was a sewing machine operator at a state school for mentally disabled children until reaching the retirement requirement.

Because Miss A.H.'s small pension and social security are not adequate for her daily living expenses, she lives with her niece. This seems to be the best option because of the cost of apartments in the community as well as difficulty in obtaining senior housing. At the senior center, which she attends daily using two buses each way, she works two days a week in the lunch room for a minimum wage. The work there is her main reason for not selecting a center closer to home.

Participant #7

Mrs. M.I., age 88, was referred to the researcher by her granddaughter, a nurse in the community. She owns the house in which she resides with her daughter and son in law on a tree-lined street in a residential neighborhood. The front door entrance to her neatly kept home has about five steps.

The living room is uncluttered showing a marked absence of pictures, papers, or personal objects. This is unusual since she has lived in the same house for fifty years. Very tidy in her appearance, she has difficulty getting around even with a walker. Hunched over, she finds it particularly hard to rise from sitting positions.

Mrs. M.I. related a childhood of economic struggle during her early years in New York City. Her father's death when she was five years old created financial constraint, leaving her mother to become the mainstay of support for the family. The woman took in wash and ironing, later remarrying a man whom Mrs. M.I. did not care for.

After attending business school she found a job at the telephone company while still in her teens and remained there until meeting her husband with whom she had three children, two girls and a boy. When he became ill in her thirties, she returned to work and continued on the job until retiring with a pension at age 65.

Social security also sustains her while her daughter and son–in–law cover most of the household expenses. Although she would prefer to live alone, she knows it is unlikely in light of her limited vision and immobility.

Prior to her other daughter's death six years earlier, Mrs. M.I. was able to leave her home regularly. At present, she can manage this activity only about once a month. She would prefer to go out more often, particularly to play Bingo at the local church if transportation were more readily available. One of her great pleasures is having breakfast with her grandson who brings food to her from McDonalds.

Participant #8

Mrs. B.J. age 85 and the youngest participant in the study, was first interviewed in a small room off the recreational hall at a senior center outside of New York City. Slightly overweight, she was dressed in a bright blue dress with matching earrings and necklace. She appeared to walk with a steady gait without assistive devices.

Born in New York City, she attended a church school for eight years and then took a factory job for a national company until she married at twenty. She continued to work at a sewing job for the next five years at which time she had her first child. After the second daughter was born and when her children were ready for school, she returned to work at a plant while her sister–in–law helped with child care. She receives social security but no pension although she was employed for more than twenty years.

When her husband died thirteen years ago, Mrs. B.J. moved into her widowed daughter's home. She seems pleased with the arrangement because she can help in looking after the house. Able to perform housekeeping chores, she also cooks dinner for her daughter.

Mrs. B.J. attends the center four days a week, made possible by the available transportation. Her mobility appears adequate for most physical activities but a cardiac condition slows her down at times.

Participant #9

Mrs. R.K., age 92, came to the researcher's attention through a friend. The interview took place in Northern New Jersey in a single family ranch home where the participant has lived with her daughter for the past twelve years. The interior of the house is readily accessible to her so that she can ambulate with the aid of a walker. After walking a short distance, however, she seems to get shortness of breath. Also, her voice appears hoarse which she claims is due to a throat surgery performed during the previous year.

Wearing sneakers, Mrs. R.K. is dressed neatly in a pale blue sweat suit. The house looks clean revealing many personal objects. There are several piles of paper in the living room and dining room, which also contains the crafts that she is working on for the church fair as well as for her family. The best part of her day, she claims, is when her daughter returns from work. Her son's regular visits strengthen her support system, even though he lives in another city with his wife and two children.

Mrs. R.K. attended school up through the tenth grade and then worked as a milliner. After her marriage, she was employed at a friend's dry goods store but not on a steady basis. A widow for the past thirty years, she lived alone for a while. She notes that she is able to manage on her social security.

At present, Mrs. R.K. goes to the senior center three days a week where she particularly enjoys doing ceramics. Her concern is that center transportation may be decreased to two days a week. Since she had a stroke two years ago, public transportation is not an option. Her visits to the center are critical to her maintaining independence.

Participant #10

Mrs R.B, age 85 and a widow for the past three years, lives alone in a two-family house that she owns. Her income comes from social security, her late husband's pension, and rent from the tenant in the upstairs apartment. The researcher knew the participant previously from home care visits made during the husband's illness. Bedridden for several years he was cared for by his wife. They had been married 55 years.

Mrs. R.B. maintains a neat and uncluttered home. She prepares all her own meals and cooks dinner for her brother and sister who visit at least once a week. She still drives her own car, accompanied by her tenant who helps with carrying the groceries. Although she required no assistive devices in walking, she admits tiring more easily and hires outside people to do yard work and other chores. She still continues to do her own housework. Her social needs seem to be met by attending church functions but she does not participate in any senior group activity. During the winter, she rarely goes outside if there is snow or ice because of her fear of falling.

Mrs. R.B. always wanted to be a nurse but when her father committed suicide, she had to leave school at age 16 to help her mother with the care of her three siblings. She married at 27 years of age and adopted a five-year old girl ten years later, whom she maintains close ties with and sees regularly.

Participant #11

Mrs. P.M., age 92, continues to live in the same house where she began her married life 71 years ago. In 1988 she lost her husband who was 96 and appears to be still grieving for him. Her one daughter, now in her sixties, calls daily and visits at least once a week. She would be willing to take her mother to a senior center, but Mrs.P.M. does not wish to do so, even though she seems physically able. The participant, who lives alone, has minimal social contacts. Apparently, her life evolved around her husband and the loss has affected her deeply.

Her home, which has an upstairs and downstairs, is neat and nicely decorated. The main level is spacious, providing for safety as well as accessibility to whatever she needs. She can do some light housekeeping but her daughter takes care of the more difficult tasks. Mrs.P. uses an electric chair lift that makes it easier to go to the upstairs level where she sleeps.

During the interview she looks tidy, dressed in a bright blue frock and wearing white leather sneakers. A cane helps her to navigate more easily, but arising from a sitting position gives her some difficulty. Financial matters are of no great concern because she receives social security and has savings in the bank from her husband. Also her daughter will offer any added assistance if needed.

Participant #12

Mrs. N.N., age 92, attends the senior center five days a week where she does not participate in any of the crafts but "enjoys watching." She sits alone at a table with her walker next to her with a small bag tied to it. A woman of average size, she has markedly swollen feet extending up to her knees. Because she lives in an apartment in the senior center complex, the proximity and elevator availability make it possible for her to go the center itself.

Born in Italy, Mrs. N. completed elementary school and then worked in a family store. She married when she was eighteen and by age 25 had three children. Shortly thereafter, the family came to the United States. During World War II, her two sons died, a tragedy which greatly affected her husband's health resulting in his death when he was forty six. Mrs. N.N. went to work to support her daughter and herself. For twenty four years she had a job sewing in a factory, which helped to provide for the girl's college education. The pension she later received and her social security help to sustain her lifestyle, which involves her three-room apartment in low cost housing and low cost meals taken at the center. Her daughter visits once a week bringing some necessary groceries.

Participant #13

Mrs. O.P. age 89, has lived for sixty years in her own home, a two family house situated on a quiet street in an old neighborhood. She spends most of her day in a wheelchair, rarely going out except for appointments with her physician or an important family event. Homebound most of the time, she reads, takes care of her bills, and plays the piano at least once a day for her own enjoyment.

The house has three steps to the front entrance and a ramp at the side entrance. A woman comes in daily to help out. Any potential obstacles have been removed. At night when Mrs. O.P. is alone, she sleeps in a hospital bed and uses a commode rather than going to the lavatory.

Born in New York City, she attended school through the tenth grade. She married, had three children and then returned to work, mainly bookkeeping, until age 60. The family is supportive, including grandchildren, who visit her often. She receives social security and a small pension from her late husband's employment. Other income comes from the rent charged to her tenant in the apartment upstairs.

Participant #14

Mrs. A.Q., age 89, is eager to live in the housing project accessible to the senior center she attends (she has applied). In her present facility — six blocks from the neighborhood, her expenses exceed the income she receives from social security. Although her children help to cover the rent of $650 a month, she would like to obtain low cost housing so that she can manage on her own.

At the age of 16, Mrs. A.Q. came from Italy with her parents and ten siblings. After completing eight grade, she worked for her father in the store he owned. She married at eighteen and has a daughter and a son, and after that she no longer took any job outside the home. In her present circumstances, she is able to care for her apartment though her gait is a little unsteady even with a cane. When her daughter visits, she brings the groceries.

Participant #15

Mrs. M.R., age 89, resides in the same house — built in the 1930's — in which she raised her six children, of whom five are living. The location is a dead end street, bordered by a swamp on one side. In the rear is a garden which produces vegetables for her and her family. She liked to bake her own bread and cans tomatoes for use in the winter.

Her life, which she describes as fulfilling, has focused on her home and children. Originally from Italy, where she characterized her early years, married at sixteen and had her first child a year later. Although she didn't want to leave her country, she joined her husband in the United States a few years later. She has never worked outside the home.

Mrs. M.R.'s support system appears strong with someone visiting every day and taking care of any special need. She attends family events but not any outside social functions. The children arrange any contacts.

She is a neat though plainly dressed woman, able to cook all her own meals as well as handle light housekeeping chores. Although she does not use a cane, she seems to have some difficulty climbing stairs.

Participant #16

Mrs. O.L., age 87 and a widow for the past 20 years, moved into her present apartment at the senior center complex thirteen years ago to be near her daughter. She described her home or "little place" as beautiful. There were three rooms which appeared to be on the dark side although it was bright outdoors. In addition to the slightly worn furniture, various papers rested on the kitchen table and on a smaller table next to the sofa.

Mrs. O.L.'s dress looked faded and a little wrinkled. Her feet were swollen and her skin dry. She used a walker at home as well as at the center but did not ambulate well even with this device.

Up until five years ago, she claims that she could do everything herself. At that time, she gave up driving and now depends on her daughter for shopping as well as transportation for health care. She is able to perform light cleaning and washing. Although Mrs. O.L. no longer cooks for herself, she reheats the food. Every day she has lunch at the center and a sandwich for supper, but her daughter often brings meals to the house. She would like to eat out for lunch but is fearful of incontinence as well as the awkwardness of using a walker.

Originally from Germany, she came to the United States as a youngster with her family who were comfortable financially, She graduated from high school — a fact of great pride to her. Married at

24, she had a son and daughter. She left her first husband because of his infidelity and later remarried. Throughout her married life, she worked as a clerk on Wall Street until forced to retire at age 70.

Participant #17

Mrs. M.S., age 89 and a widow, remains the only survivor in a family of six. She admits that her main reason for coming to the senior center is to be with people. All her friends are dead and she has no children of her own. Her only support systems appear to be the center staff and a godchild whom she only seeks out in a time of crisis.

Mrs. M.S. tires easily but is able to walk without assistive devices. By resting between activities, she can accomplish most of her daily tasks such as cleaning her own apartment and taking care of herself. She relies on the center bus service for shopping, and for help with bills, if needed, from the director. However, finances represent a big concern, particularly in light of recent medical costs that she is unable to pay. Although the apartment rent is low at the senior center complex, her present expenses exceed her social security income, the only source of financial support.

Participant #18

Mrs. A.T., age 88, is an independent woman who continues to be active in church affairs and even models for shows! At the senior center, she engages actively in its functions and encourages others to participate. Although a fractured hip five years ago limited her activities, particularly her dancing, she considers going out and talking with people as very important to her.

Born in New York City, she was one of five children. When she was eight years old, her father deserted the family and her grandmother came to live with them. She attended a one-room school house until turning 15 and then took jobs picking vegetables, cleaning houses and working in a night club. At 17, she married and had five children, of whom three are living. After leaving her alcoholic husband, she worked as a saleswoman in a department store where she remained until reaching 65-years of age.

Although the job gave no pension, Mrs. A.T. was able to save money which later in life provided her with some financial security.

She also depends upon social security and thus can manage her situation since her rent is low in the subsidized housing where she lives.

She sees her sons regularly but does not appear to depend upon them. With available car service, she does her own shopping and is able to cook if she desires to do so. During the week, however, she eats most of her meals at the senior center.

Participant #19

Mrs. M.M., age 105, the oldest participant in the study lives in a suburb of New York City in a small house located in a modest complex that at one time was a group of homes used as a summer camp. The arrangement provides for privacy as well as security. Her neighbors watch over her carefully. Two steps lead to the interior of the house which appears cozy and warm, and is filled with objects easily accessible.

Although Mrs. M.M. is bent over, and appears to have some difficulty walking even with a walker, she does not seem to be frail. She is handicapped by no vision in her left eye and partial loss in the right one. Yet, she can prepare her own breakfast, and heat food, wash her clothes, and hang them on a backyard line in good weather. Until recently, she was able to use her sewing machine. At present, a handy man performs some of the cleaning and yard work as well as other activities she can no longer do.

Born in Nova Scotia, Mrs. M.M. was eight years old when her mother died and she came to New York to live with an aunt who raised her. She studied to become a registered nurse and enlisted in the U.S. Army Nurse Corps for two years. For a long time she remained active in the American Legion and her nursing school's alumnae association. She continues an interest in her church and is visited regularly by some of the members, including a young family.

When she was 57, Mrs. M.M. entered into her first marriage, which lasted for eighteen years until her husband died. The only relatives she sees occasionally are her nieces and nephews since they do not live nearby. Her financial situation seems adequate as she has some savings and receives social security. She owns her own home and can afford outside services when needed. Through its nutrition

program, the town's senior center arranges to bring her a hot lunch
and sandwich daily.

Participant #20

Mrs. N.M., age 92 and a widow for forty years, lives in a senior
center complex with access to the services and activities of the center.
Yet, she does not seem to take advantage of the various offerings,
which is reflected by her lack of participation in either a single activity
or group activities. She appears to be quite dependent on her daughter
but doesn't want to be a burden.

Mrs.N.M. emigrated from Italy when she was eight years old.
After finishing eight years of schooling, she began to work as a sewing
machine operator in a factory. At 19, she married and had two
children, one of whom died in World War II. Through the years, she
supported herself taking on various sewing jobs. One of her fears in
her older years is that she will not be able to live on her own without
help from her daughter. The eventual possibility of a nursing home
also worries her.

Mrs.N.M. uses a can but seems unsteady when she walks. She
has her lunch at the center and a sandwich for dinner unless her
daughter brings in a hot meal. She does not feel safe cooking at the
stove, but is able to do a small wash in the sink. Although her
apartment's rent is low she received social security, it is difficult for
her to meet daily living expenses intensified by medical costs
including medication.

Appendix B

THE INTERVIEW GUIDE

1. How do you spend your day?

2. How did you spend your day at age 20, 40, and 60?

3. How do you vary your day according to seasons?

4. What part of your day is most important to you?

5. What comes to mind when you think of activity?

6. Are there activities that you no longer engage in?

7. What was the reason for giving up certain activities?

8. Which activities did you find hardest to give up?

9. What do you think stopped you from doing certain activities?

10. What or who influenced what activities have been performed throughout your life?

11. What new activities have you taken on as time passed?

12. If given the opportunity, how would you choose to spend your day now?

13. Describe a *perfect* day.

14. How do you feel about your life now?

Index